WRITTEN AND PHOTOGRAPHED
BY RODNEY HYETT

THE GREAT OCEAN ROAD

A TRAVELLER'S GUIDE

GREAT OCEAN PUBLICATIONS

First published in 1995 by
Great Ocean Publications
Currells Road, Port Campbell, Victoria, 3269
Telephone 055 986 203

Edited by Tom Williams
Designed by Rodney Hyett
Cartography by Mercadier, Canberra
Colour separations by Markbys Renaissance, Port Melbourne
Printed by Incolour Printing, Moorabbin
Bound by M & M Binders, Mount Waverley

ISBN 0 646 21220 6

CONTENTS

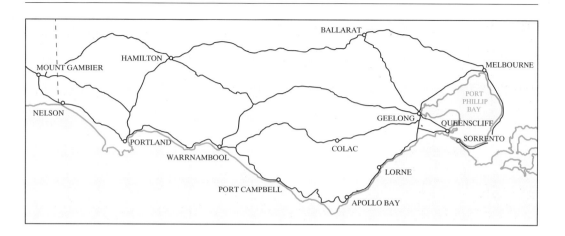

INTRODUCTION

It was not until the late 1980s that the endlessly-snaking dirt road across Cape Otway was finally redirected and bitumenized. It cut a bold new pass through the Otway Ranges that easily connected the two stretches of coastline on either side of the cape, thereby creating the extended Great Ocean Road as we know it today, arguably the finest scenic coastal drive in the world. Significantly, substantial parts of the coastline were made state and national parks, thus reducing the opportunity for excessive development and commercialization. The lack of a warmly seductive climate has perhaps played its part as well in preserving the natural environment. There is the Big Tree, there are big waves and plenty of big cliffs, but fortunately no plastic replicas of the Twelve Apostles.

This magnificent tract of untamed coastline provides us all with a chance to return to the simple enjoyment of nature, and its relationship with us that is otherwise lost in our mechanized world. Here, at times, the forces of nature are potently expressed. They can give an injection of vitality to lift the body and soul, they can take you on a journey with which no magic carpet ride through virtual reality can compete. Whatever the conditions, tempestuous fury in winter or idyllic calm in autumn, the Great Ocean Road presents a geographic feast to relish. Here you are confronted by a geology immense in time and scale, whether drawn from dinosaur bones of eons ago or London Bridge's collapse of recent times.

This book concentrates on revealing the natural wonders and pleasures of the Great Ocean Road rather than the commercial diversions. For enthusiasts of the great outdoors the attractions of this coastline can exceed all expectations. It provides outstanding opportunities for bushwalking, camping, surfing and fishing, to mention but a few of its delights. And all are possible in as isolated an environment as you choose to seek out. Accommodation is equally broad in its variety and degree

of seclusion. Indeed, there seems to be an ever-growing demand for alternatives to mainstream motels and flats, judging by the mushrooming of cottages and bed-and-breakfasts along the Great Ocean Road. Sixty of these places have been carefully selected and photographed, of which only one is actually modern, the others being more rustic, if not quaint.

The book is designed to provide a summation of all the townships along the Great Ocean Road and to present them in a manner whereby comparisons are easy to make. To a large extent it is designed for people with little knowledge of this area, whether they be from interstate or overseas. The attractions and facilities listed at the bottom of each township page are often further detailed in the directory at the back of the book. Their scope grew a little in the course of compilation, so I hope it will even be useful to local residents of the Great Ocean Road. There is a limit, however, as to how much comprehensive information a book of this kind can impart on all topics. It is intended to be supplemented with specific information and detailed maps of local areas, all of which are readily available from the appropriate tourist information centres, Conservation and Natural Resources offices, or sometimes, the local shire.

For over 25 years I have travelled the greater part of this coast, surfing its waves. As a professional photographer now living in its midst, I have had the opportunity to explore its depths even further and capture its varied tones on film. Experiencing the ocean in all its moods is, to me, an endless pleasure. It can have an almost therapeutic quality. It can be an elixir for life's complexities. This magical ribbon of ocean road throws life open to new encounters for which travelling must be the greatest source, especially when that marvellous element of chance appears along the way. I hope this book is a useful guide and an inducement to make the journey and search a little further.

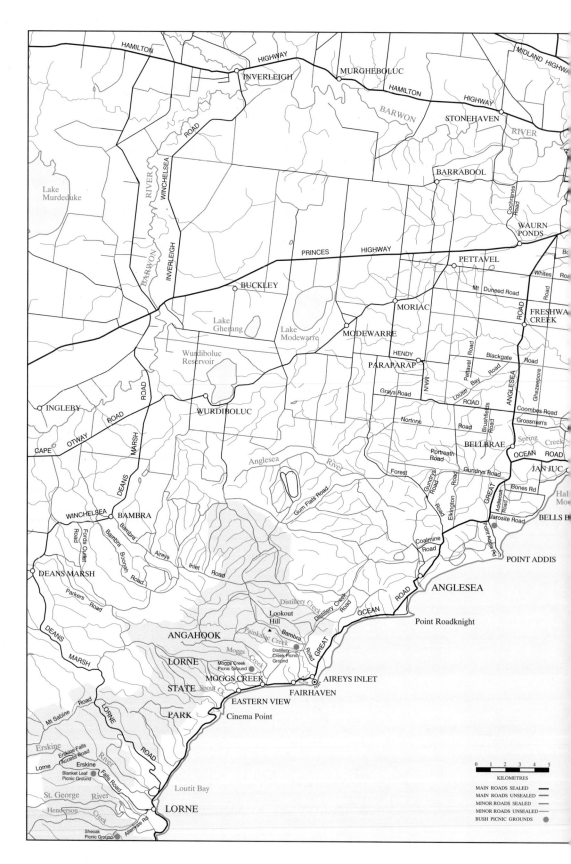

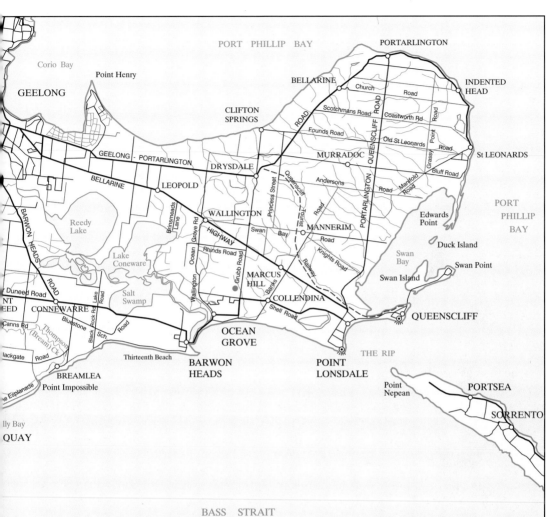

QUEENSCLIFF TO LORNE

QUEENSCLIFF

A popular seaside resort late last century, Queenscliff has been restored to its former glory and reputation for lavish hospitality. Among the most notable are the sumptuous restorations of the Queenscliff Hotel and Vue Grand Private Hotel. Situated on a narrow headland within Port Phillip Bay, Queenscliff is surrounded by calm waters and it is surprising that it should have a lighthouse at all, let alone two magnificent specimens. In fact, they are necessary indicators for a ship's safe passage through Port Phillip Heads, assisted by pilot boats based at Queenscliff. Historically this area was of strategic importance for naval defence, indeed the first artillery shot fired by the British Empire in World War I was on order from Fort Queenscliff. From Point Nepean the shot was aimed across the stern of a German freighter escaping the bay. Today Queenscliff serves as home to the Australian Army Staff College. A substantial fishing fleet and ferry service to Sorrento are located at the wharf, creating a focus of activity for the township and its stream of sea-borne visitors.

ATTRACTIONS

Bellarine Peninsula Steam Railway museum and operating railway

Community Market held on the last Sunday of the month

Fishing Fleet and wharf

Ferry Services across Port Phillip Bay to the Mornington Peninsula

Fort Queenscliff Museum and guided tours of the fort

Lighthouses one is black (the only bluestone lighthouse in Australia), the other is white

Marine Discovery Centre educational displays of marine life, open during school holidays

Queenscliff Historical Centre local history

Queenscliff Maritime Centre & Museum

Swan Bay and Swan Island prolific bird life in the bay and golf course on the island

Population.....................................1650	Aquarium	Picnic Ground	Churches (3)
Distance from Melbourne (km)...105	Art Gallery	Playground	Newsagent
Hotels 5	Boat Charter	Safe Swimming-	Petrol Station
Motel 1	Craft Shop	beach	Police Station
Caravan Parks....................................5	Diving	Squash Courts	Post Office
Cottages / Bed & Breakfast..............5	Golf Course	Sunday Market	RACV
Flats & Units 12	Historical Society	Tea-rooms	Supermarket
Guest Houses.....................................4	Jetty	Tennis Courts	Take Away Food
Hostel / Backpackers.........................1	Lawn Bowls	Bank	Toilets
Host Farm 1	Lighthouse	Boat Ramp	Tourist Info.
Restaurants 10	Museum	EFTPOS	

POINT LONSDALE

Nestled behind sand dunes and amongst thick tea tree, Point Lonsdale is positioned on Port Phillip Heads overlooking the notorious Rip, through which all Melbourne and Geelong shipping must pass. Scenic interest tends to be focused around the heads. The most conspicuous landmark is the lighthouse, with Buckley's Cave just below it in the cliff, which was supposedly the home of William Buckley early last century. He escaped from a convict settlement at Sorrento in 1803, aged 23, and later spent some thirty years dwelling with the local aborigines, who took him to be a returned spirit because of his fair skin. Buckley was eventually given a free pardon in 1835 and died in Tasmania at the age of 76, after a fall from a horse. There are two beaches at Point Lonsdale, a protected one inside the heads and the main surf beach around the corner. It tends to be quiet and residential, compared with its close and more commercial neighbour Queenscliff. A restful spot, where simply watching the ships pass through the heads must be a nautical person's ideal pastime.

ATTRACTIONS
Buckley's Cave below the lighthouse
Front Beach and grassy foreshore for picnicing
Jetty for fishing
Lighthouse
Marconi Memorial where the first overseas broadcast by radio was made in 1906
Port Phillip Heads and The Rip with views of Point Nepean

Population 1800	Craft Shop	Surfing	Take Away Food
Distance from Melbourne (km)...102	Diving	Tennis Courts	Toilets
Hotel ....-	Golf Course	EFTPOS	
Motels...2	Jetty	Churches (2)	
Caravan Parks..................................3	Lawn Bowls	General Store	
Cottages / Bed & Breakfast..............2	Lighthouse	Medical Centre	
Flats & Units 10	Picnic Ground	Newsagent	
Guest House 1	Playground	Petrol Station	
Hostel / Backpackers.........................-	Safe Swimming-	Police Station	
Host Farm ....-	beach	Post Office	
Restaurant...1	Sunday Market	SLSC Patrols	

OCEAN GROVE

An ever-expanding town, Ocean Grove overlooks the tranquil Barwon River as well as sandy ocean beaches. Between the two is a narrow and naturally sheltered foreshore reserve for camping, stretching nearly two kilometres. Upstream is the Lake Connewarre State Game Reserve, including the marshland of Reedy Lake, the latter providing a good breeding habitat for water birds. The reserve is a feeding ground to the extremely rare orange bellied parrot during the winter months. The lakes are generally too shallow for boating but perfect for canoeing and windsurfing. By an interesting quirk of fate, Ocean Grove has never had a hotel until relatively recently. Late last century, Methodist missionaries from Ocean Grove in New Jersey bought up large areas of land for a sanatorium that failed to eventuate. Subsequently the land was resold, but with covenants prohibiting the manufacture or sale of alcohol. Luckily Barwon Heads served as a nearby watering-hole.

ATTRACTIONS
Barwon River Estuary and prolific birdlife
Foreshore Camping 750 sites
Moorfield Wildlife Park
Lake Connewarre canoeing and windsurfing
Ocean Grove Nature Reserve natural bushland park
Safe Ocean Beaches

Population.....................................7000	Art Gallery	Safe Swimming-	Boat Ramp	Take Away Food
Distance from Melbourne (km).....98	Bushwalking	beach	Churches (3)	Toilets
Hotel..1	Canoeing	Squash Courts	EFTPOS	Tourist Info.
Motels...4	Craft Shop	Sunday Market	Medical Centre	
Caravan Parks....................................6	Diving	Surfing	Newsagent	
Cottages / Bed & Breakfast..............8	Golf Course	Tea-rooms	Petrol Station	
Flats & Units 20	Gymnasium	Tennis Courts	Police Station	
Guest House.......................................-	Horse Trail Rides	Wildlife Park	Post Office	
Hostel / Backpackers.........................-	Lawn Bowls	Autogas	RACV	
Host Farm ....-	Picnic Ground	ATM	SLSC Patrols	
Restaurants 8	Playground	Bank	Supermarket	

BARWON HEADS

Compared to its Ocean Grove twin, Barwon Heads is a lot more sedate, being located downstream a little, right at the mouth of the Barwon River. Spanning the estuary is one of the few wooden bridges of significance still remaining along the Great Ocean Road. It is some three hundred metres long and always dotted with fishermen. A craggy headland called the Bluff protects a sandy river beach, whilst just around the corner Thirteenth Beach has rolling surf along its endless stretch. Tucked behind the sand dunes of Thirteenth lies the Barwon Heads Golf Club with its eighteen-hole links, reminiscent of the great Scottish courses. There is also a nine-hole practice course and a distinguished, seventy-year-old clubhouse, renowned for its Sunday lunches, if you can find a member to take you there. Eight kilometres south-west of the Bluff is the Ship's Graveyard, where at least twenty-five vessels lie in thirty-five fathoms, scuttled between 1925 and 1971.

ATTRACTIONS
Barwon River Estuary and prolific birdlife
Barwon Heads Golf Club
Jirrahlinga Koala & Wildlife Sanctuary
Lake Connewarre canoeing and windsurfing
The Bluff limestone headland
Thirteenth Beach for surfing

Population....................................2100	Boat Charter	Surfing	Newsagent
Distance from Melbourne (km).....96	Canoeing	Tea-rooms	Petrol Station
Hotel...1	Diving	Tennis Courts	Police Station
Motel 1	Golf Course	Wildlife Park	Post Office
Caravan Parks...................................2	River Jetty	Airfield	SLSC Patrols
Cottages / Bed & Breakfast..............-	Picnic Ground	Autogas	Supermarket
Flats & Units....................................-	Playground	Bank (agency)	Take Away Food
Guest House.....................................-	Safe Swimming-	Boat Ramps	Toilets
Hostel / Backpackers........................-	beach	Churches (3)	Tourist Info.
Host Farm ....-	Scenic Flights	EFTPOS	
Restaurant..1	Sunday Market	Medical Centre	

BREAMLEA

A quiet out-of-the-way hamlet nestled in the sand dunes, Breamlea offers few facilities and is all the more charming for it. The houses, home to a mostly permanent population, stretch out along the sand hills. Quite a few are located well into the dunes and have exceptional views towards Barwon Heads. Behind them is Bancoora surf beach, an exposed stretch of shoreline, whilst on the other side are the wetlands and the prolific birdlife of Thompson Creek. It is locally and more aptly known as Bream Creek, meandering through the flats, then losing itself completely in the reeds before finding the ocean at Point Impossible. Best known as a surfing spot, Point Impossible is actually a spot where everything is possible since wearing nothing is optional. It's on the Torquay side of the point, should you be wondering (or wandering). On a more mundane level, Breamlea makes the claim of having the surf beach that lies closest to Melbourne on the Great Ocean Road.

ATTRACTIONS
Bancoora Surf Beach
Bird Life of Thompson Creek wetlands
Point Impossible

Population	100	Bushwalking	SLSC Patrols
Distance from Melbourne (km)	92	Diving	Take Away Food
Hotel	-	Picnic Ground	Toilets
Motel	-	Playground	
Caravan Park	1	Safe Swimming-	
Cottages / Bed & Breakfast	-	beach	
Flats & Units	-	Surfing	
Guest House	-	General Store	
Hostel / Backpackers	-	Newsagent	
Host Farm	-	Petrol	
Restaurant	-	Post Office	

TORQUAY

Torquay is a popular, bustling town that has developed dramatically over the last few years, mainly around the surfing industry and its myriad businesses, the grandfathers of them all being Rip Curl and Quiksilver. These two companies have a combined annual turnover in the order of one hundred million dollars. There are three main beaches: the more rugged back beach for surf, then the gracious and protected front beach lined with Norfolk pines, and finally Fishermans beach, which is more often than not completely becalmed. The town is connected to Geelong by the new Surf Coast Highway that leads straight to the Surf Coast Plaza, which is quite close to the recently created Surf Coast Shire. With names like those, there is no doubt about the town's identity or focus. Neighbouring Jan Juc (derived from the Aboriginal word for ironbark) is almost entirely a residential suburb of Torquay, with a wonderful cliff-lined beach and surf life saving club of its own.

ATTRACTIONS
Point Danger lookout and great windsurfing spot
Surf Coast Plaza extensive retail centre for the surfing industry, including surfwear fashion

Surfworld Museum including interactive videos and historic surf movies
Taylors Park natural parkland & large playground opposite
Variety of Beaches catering for all water sports

Population.................................5000	Art Gallery	Safe Swimming-	Boat Ramp	Take Away Food
Distance from Melbourne (km).....96	Bushwalking	beach	Churches (4)	Toilets
Hotels 2	Craft Shop	Scenic Flights	EFTPOS	Tourist Info.
Motels...3	Diving	Sunday Market	Medical Centre	
Caravan Parks....................................4	Golf Course	Surfing	Newsagent	
Cottages / Bed & Breakfast............12	Gymnasium	Tea-rooms	Petrol Station	
Flats & Units 45	Horse Trail Rides	Tennis Courts	Police Station	
Guest House 1	Lawn Bowls	Airfield	Post Office	
Hostel / Backpackers........................-	Museum	Autogas	RACV	
Host Farms..4	Picnic Ground	ATM	SLSC Patrols	
Restaurants 12	Playground	Bank	Supermarket	

BELLS BEACH

At this point along the coast, bushland becomes more a feature of the landscape with a visually pleasing blend of pasture and bush, gently undulating. The Bells Beach Surfing Reserve was proclaimed by the state government in 1973, the first of its kind in the world. It is a unique location focused around the cliff-lined beach of Bells and flanked by two other breaks within the reserve: the always popular Winkipop, and Centreside. Bells is by far and away the most surfed area in Victoria, and with its ability to hold large swells is home to the prestigious Bells Easter Surfing Competition. This is the longest running professional surfing contest in the world and commenced in 1962. It's a powerful image, often seen from here, when off-shore winds and large swells give form to the ocean's energy, sweeping past in great arcs down the coast. Most cleansing and invigorating for all concerned.

Art Gallery (outside the reserve), Bushwalking, Diving, Picnic Ground, Surfing, Toilets

POINT ADDIS

Apart from the odd farmhouse, Point Addis is an unsettled area with a remote feeling and spectacular setting. To the north of the car park and lookout is the protected and cliff-lined beach that stretches in a long, perfect arc towards Bells Beach. A forty minute walk along this beach takes you to Southside, another designated area euphemistically known as an "optional dress beach". South of Point Addis is another more exposed stretch of sandy beach (exposed that is, to nature more than to naturalists), and accessible via a meandering walkway that starts at the carpark. Within the surrounding bushland at Point Addis is the Ironbark Basin Reserve. It has several walking tracks through natural bushland, replete with birdlife, assorted native creatures and scenic views. The reserve includes a picnic ground with BBQs and is partially accessible to wheelchairs.

Bushwalking, Diving, Picnic Ground, Safe Swimming Beach, Surfing

ANGLESEA

At the foothills of the Otway Ranges, Anglesea is surrounded by bush. Just behind the town, but completely concealed, is Alcoa's power station, fuelled by brown coal from an open-cut mine. The township begins around the Anglesea River estuary and its wide grassy banks, then sprawls into the hills to be mostly consumed by the bush. The beach, though concealed from view by sand dunes, is one of the town's main attractions and continues around to Point Roadknight. This adjoining residential area with its own vast beach is protected by the slender rocky spine of Point Roadknight. As with Torquay, Ocean Grove and Lorne, Anglesea's population swells phenomenally during the summer holidays, mostly with campers injecting a good deal of colour and movement. Equally, the golf course puts on an entertaining display with its resident population of kangaroos. The putting-greens can get fairly crowded, however you rarely lose a ball on this well grazed course.

ATTRACTIONS
Anglesea Golf Course and kangaroos
Alcoa Power Station access is restricted to lookout points in Coalmine Road and Camp Road
Coogoorah Park adventure park in a bushland setting
Native Orchids seen in the Bald Hills area during Spring
Point Roadknight headland and beach

Population 1850	Art Gallery	Playground	Medical Centre
Distance from Melbourne (km)...112	Bushwalking	Safe Swimming-	Newsagent
Hotel...1	Canoeing	beach	Petrol Station
Motels...3	Craft Shop	Surfing	Police Station
Caravan Parks....................................3	Diving	Tea-rooms	Post Office
Cottages / Bed & Breakfast..............7	Golf Course	Tennis Courts	RACV
Flats & Units 10	Historical Society	ATM	SLSC Patrols
Guest House 1	Horse Trail Rides	Bank	Supermarket
Hostel / Backpackers........................-	River Jetty	Boat Ramp	Take Away Food
Host Farm ....-	Lawn Bowls	Churches (3)	Toilets
Restaurants.......................................2	Picnic Ground	EFTPOS	Tourist Info.

AIREYS INLET

Though largely burnt out by the Ash Wednesday fire in 1983, Aireys Inlet has now completely recovered its former delightful character. The Painkalac Creek estuary snakes around the flats below the town, before a dramatic entry into the ocean, flanked by sandstone cliffs. The local geography provides for great fossicking and rock-pooling along a variety of cliff-lined beaches. The volcano responsible for it all erupted over thirty million years ago. The Angahook Lorne State Park, an integral part of the Otway Ranges, begins at Aireys Inlet, extending along the coast to Kennett River. Vegetation ranges from rainforest to heathland according to rainfall. In fact, the heathland around Aireys (and Anglesea for that matter) is regarded as one of the most significant floras in the state, boasting orchids of international renown. They are a blaze of colour in spring.

ATTRACTIONS
Angahook Lorne State Park
Allen Noble Sanctuary for waterbirds
Distillery Creek Picnic Ground BBQs and bushwalking
Native Orchids in the surrounding heathland during Spring
The Bark Hut replica of an early settlers hut
Split Point Lighthouse with walking tracks and lookouts

Population....................................680	Art Gallery	State Park	Post Office
Distance from Melbourne (km)...122	Bushwalking	Surfing	Take Away Food
Hotel..1	Canoeing	Tea-rooms	Toilets
Motel..1	Craft Shop	Tennis Courts	
Caravan Park.................................1	Diving	Bank (agency)	
Cottages / Bed & Breakfast.............8	Horse Trail Rides	Boat Ramp	
Flats & Units.................................5	Lighthouse	Church	
Guest House....................................-	Picnic Ground	General Store	
Hostel / Backpackers.......................-	Playground	Medical Centre	
Host Farm.......................................1	Safe Swimming-	Newsagent	
Restaurants.....................................2	beach	Petrol Station	

FAIRHAVEN TO EASTERN VIEW

Just around the corner from Aireys Inlet is Fairhaven, at the beginning of a six kilometre dead-straight stretch of magnificent beach ending at Eastern View and including Moggs Creek. Fairhaven is more a residential annexation of Aireys Inlet, divided from it only by Painkalac Creek, whereas Moggs Creek is a tiny settlement in its own right. There are whispers of it being an artists' colony. Dotted along this section of coast and above the road are an interesting collection of new houses, spawned by the Ash Wednesday fire of 1983 and all taking in the panoramic views. The Memorial Arch at Eastern View marks the start of the Great Ocean Road's truly majestic journey, from here on dramatically hugging the coastline along its way. A plaque on the arch proclaims the road was built to commemorate the services of those who served in World War I.

ATTRACTIONS
Angahook Lorne State Park
Hang Glider Launching Pad at Moggs Creek
Great Ocean Road Memorial Arch first built in 1939 and
completely rebuilt after the Ash Wednesday fires, but on
the original stone supports
Moggs Creek Picnic Reserve and bushwalks

Population....................................200	
Distance from Melbourne (km)...126	
Hotel...................................-	
Motel...................................-	
Caravan Park.............................-	
Cottages / Bed & Breakfast.............-	
Flats & Units...........................-	
Guest House.............................-	
Hostel / Backpackers....................-	
Host Farm...............................-	
Restaurant..............................-	

Art Gallery   SLSC Patrols
Bushwalking   Toilets
Craft Shop
Diving
Hang Gliding
Horse Trail Rides
Picnic Ground
Safe Swimming-
beach
State Park
Surfing

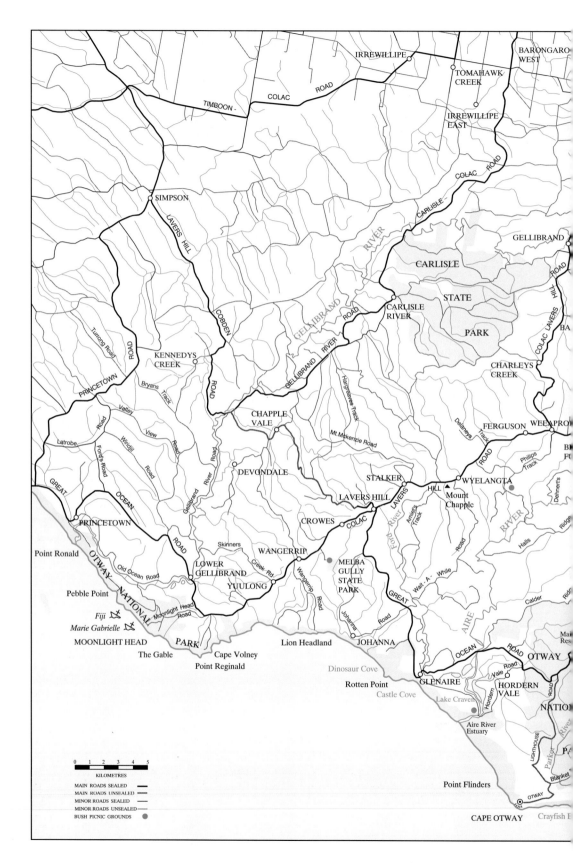

IRREWILLIPE

BARONGARO WEST

TOMAHAWK CREEK

IRREWILLIPE EAST

TIMBOON - COLAC ROAD

COLAC ROAD

GELLIBRAND

SIMPSON

CARLISLE

RIVER

CARLISLE STATE PARK

LAVERS HILL

CARLISLE -

CARLISLE RIVER

COLAC LAVERS HILL

BA

COBDEN

KENNEDYS CREEK

GELLIBRAND RIVER ROAD

GELLIBRAND RIVER

CHARLEYS CREEK

Turong Road

PRINCETOWN ROAD

Bryans Track

ROAD

Hargreaves Track

Delaneys Track

FERGUSON

WEEAPRO

Valley

View

Windill

Road

Road

ROAD

Road

CHAPPLE VALE

Mt.Mckenzie Road

ROAD

Philips Track

B FO

Latrobe

Fords Road

Gellibrand River Road

River Road

DEVONDALE

STALKER

HILL

Mount Chapple

WYELANGTA

Dehnert's

GREAT

OCEAN

LAVERS HILL

LAVERS River

Amier's Track

Ridge

Halls

PRINCETOWN

Old Ocean Road

ROAD

Skinners

Creek - Rd

CROWES COLAC

WANGERRIP

Wangerrip Road

MELBA GULLY STATE PARK

Road

RIVER

Point Ronald

OTWAY

LOWER GELLIBRAND

YUULONG

GREAT

Wait - A - While

AIRE

Calder

Ridg

Pebble Point

Fiji

Marie Gabrielle

MOONLIGHT HEAD

NATIONAL

Moonlight Head Road

Johanna Road

OCEAN

Road

OTWAY

Mai Res

PARK

The Gable

Cape Volney

Point Reginald

Lion Headland

JOHANNA

ROAD

NATIOI

Dinosaur Cove

GLENAIRE

Vale Road

HORDERN VALE

P

Rotten Point

Castle Cove

Lake Craven

Hordern Road

Aire River Estuary

LIGHTHOUSE

Parker River

Blanket

Point Flinders

OTWAY

CAPE OTWAY

Crayfish B

0 1 2 3 4 5
KILOMETRES

MAIN ROADS SEALED
MAIN ROADS UNSEALED
MINOR ROADS SEALED
MINOR ROADS UNSEALED
BUSH PICNIC GROUNDS

LORNE TO PRINCETOWN

LORNE

Lorne is truly one of the jewels of the Great Ocean Road, a special place of enormous charm that not even recent development can spoil. At the height of summer it caters for an ever-changing and more sophisticated holiday maker, drawn to its promenade and the outdoor cafés that have enriched Lorne for so many years. During the out-of-season months, though, its intrinsic beauty is even more apparent, free from the summer swarms. Nestled in a protected cove, it is enveloped by bush with a wealth of walking tracks and waterfalls. Nearly all of these are in the Angahook Lorne State Park which seems to be at its most luxuriant in the Lorne area, especially with regard to waterfalls and cascades. Even the weather is unique, being marginally cooler than other beaches on the hottest summer days, and with a relatively mild winter, it has to my mind the best of both worlds. The beach is a delight and always crowded in summer. It has a great body-surfing wave, and at the southern end of the beach there is a rocky point-break for surfboards.

ATTRACTIONS

Angahook Lorne State Park
Blanket Leaf and Sheoak Picnic Grounds
Bushwalks and Waterfalls many and varied (see page 99)
Erskine Falls is the most famous and easily accessible

Great Otway Classic marathon in May / June
Pier and fishing boats
Pier to Pub Swim Classic in January
Qdos Art Gallery contemporary art exhibitions
Restaurants and promenade with outdoor cafés

Population 1000	Art Gallery	Playground	Boat Ramp	Supermarket
Distance from Melbourne (km)...143	Bushwalking	Safe Swimming-	Churches (3)	Take Away Food
Hotels 2	Canoeing	beach	EFTPOS	Toilets
Motels...6	Craft Shop	State Park	Hospital	Tourist Info.
Caravan Parks....................................5	Diving	Surfing	Medical Centre	
Cottages / Bed & Breakfast............30	Golf Course	Swimming Pool	Newsagent	
Flats & Units 108	Gymnasium	Tea-rooms	Petrol Station	
Guest Houses....................................2	Historical Society	Tennis Courts	Police Station	
Hostel / Backpackers........................1	Jetty	Autogas	Post Office	
Host Farms.......................................2	Lawn Bowls	ATM	RACV	
Restaurants 10	Picnic Grounds	Bank	SLSC Patrols	

CUMBERLAND RIVER

A few kilometres south-west of Lorne is a glorious camping location at the Cumberland River. Remarkably protected, it is right on the river with soaring cliffs beside. Opposite are wide lawns to the river's edge and cypress trees, in all a magnificent setting which even has its own small beach at the mouth of the river. On calmer days the ocean is safe for swimming, otherwise the river mouth provides a good wading pool. Unexpectedly there is a sizeable cave, not widely known of, called the Cumberland Cave. It is accessible from the beach, about two hundred metres west of the river mouth. Upstream from the camping ground, a three kilometre walk with a degree of rock-hopping, will bring you to a series of cascades known as Cumberland Falls. The return walk is simply a case of backtracking the same way or taking a more difficult detour via Sheoak Falls and Swallow Cave. The camping ground is closed during winter, but don't let that deter a visit, it's perfect for a picnic.

Bushwalking, Cumberland Falls, Camping & Caravan Park, Diving, Picnic Ground, Playground, State Park, Surfing, Toilets

WYE RIVER

The houses of Wye River cut into and poke up from hills even steeper than those of Lorne, providing spectacular views and good exercise. The town is located on that part of the Great Ocean Road where it clings to the coastline in the most breathtaking manner. The road snakes on endlessly, to the delight of would-be rally drivers and the despair of their queasy passengers. In fact, this section of the Great Ocean Road and that around Port Campbell are often captured on film for local and overseas car advertisements. Wye River is a small outpost compared to Lorne and a lot less developed, being overgrown as it is by nature in all her beauty. Rocky platforms are common along the shoreline near Wye River, but make way for two sandy beaches. The smaller one is at Separation Creek and the main one is around the corner, alongside the foreshore camping reserve.

ATTRACTIONS
Angahook Lorne State Park
Beaches including isolated ones in the surrounding area
Bushwalking in the Otway Ranges

Population	200	Bushwalking	Post Office
Distance from Melbourne (km)	161	Diving	SLSC Patrols
Hotel	1	Picnic Ground	Take Away Food
Motel	1	Playground	Toilets
Caravan Parks	2	Safe Swimming-	
Cottages / Bed & Breakfast	-	beach	
Flats & Units	-	State Park	
Guest House	-	Surfing	
Hostel / Backpackers	-	General Store	
Host Farm	-	Newsagent	
Restaurant	1	Petrol	

KENNETT RIVER

Five kilometres or so past Wye River is Kennett River, less obvious in its beauty, but with a charm of its own. There are more houses than residents, most being holiday places enveloped by bush and scarcely visible. Below, there is a large and protected foreshore camping reserve, serviced by a general store. Just over the road is the beach, a sheltered cove that has a great point-break wave for surfing when conditions are a bit rough elsewhere. Behind Kennett River and five kilometres or so along the Grey River Road is the Grey River Reserve, with a picnic ground beside a bridge over the river. Quite a large population of koalas inhabits this area, and you are almost guaranteed to see one along the first four kilometres of the Grey River Road, particularly on the north side of the road. Look high up in the forks of trees and on north-facing slopes.

ATTRACTIONS
Angahook Lorne State Park
Carisbrook Falls Scenic Reserve located seven kilometres
west of Kennett River along the Great Ocean Road, it is
one of the highest falls in the Otways
Grey River Reserve and picnic ground

Population	50	Bushwalking	Petrol
Distance from Melbourne (km)	166	Diving	Post Office
Hotel	-	Picnic Ground	SLSC Patrols
Motel	-	Playground	Take Away Food
Caravan Park	1	Safe Swimming-	Toilets
Cottages / Bed & Breakfast	-	beach	
Flats & Units	-	State Park	
Guest House	-	Surfing	
Hostel / Backpackers	-	Tennis Courts	
Host Farm	-	General Store	
Restaurant	-	Newsagent	

SKENES CREEK

Approaching Skenes Creek, the Great Ocean Road takes on a new geographic phase and mood. The road drops down closer to the sea and the steep hills recede a fraction, creating what has now become a strip of pasture beside the ocean. Skenes Creek tends to be thought of as a part of Apollo Bay, but is definitely a township in its own right, albeit one without a single shop. Apollo Bay is only six kilometres further on. The steep climbing roads to the inland offer panoramic views from exhilarating vantage-points, and are not to be missed. Either Skenes Creek Road or Wild Dog Road will take you dizzily up to Tanybryn then onto Beech Forest by way of the acclaimed forest drive along Turtons Track. Down below at sea level, the delightful Skenes Creek beach gently arcs between rocky points, with a protected camping ground just behind the foreshore.

ATTRACTIONS
Aire Valley Reserve camping and picnic ground
Beauchamp Falls and Hopetoun Falls
Chris's Beacon Point Restaurant

Tanybryn Teahouse and Gallery
Turtons Track famous forest drive
Wild Dog Road and Skenes Creek Road scenic drives with spectacular views

Population....................................200	Art Gallery
Distance from Melbourne (km)...181	Bushwalking
Hotel...-	Diving
Motels..2	Gymnasium
Caravan Park....................................1	Horse Trail Rides
Cottages / Bed & Breakfast.............2	Picnic Ground
Flats & Units..................................18	Safe Swimming-
Guest House.....................................1	beach
Hostel / Backpackers........................-	Surfing
Host Farm...1	Toilets
Restaurants.......................................3	

APOLLO BAY

Leisurely paced, but slowly changing in character, Apollo Bay supports the two main local industries of fishing and tourism. Past logging and farming have stripped away a lot of the surrounding bush, creating a broad sweep of pasture from the Otway foothills right down to the cypress-lined beach. These days though, there are more potters and musicians occupying the surrounding hills than dairy farmers. At one end of the bay is a breakwater with a harbour for the crayfishing fleet, then a vast sandy beach that goes on forever. The foreshore is similarly vast, with all sorts of facilities on the wide lawns. Inland are the wonderful Otway Ranges which include the Otway National Park just to the west of Apollo Bay. The park covers a large area of rainforest inland from Blanket Bay, then continues on from Cape Otway as a narrow ribbon along the coast, all the way to Princetown.

ATTRACTIONS

Bass Strait Shell Museum
Beauchamp Falls, Hopetoun Falls and Marriners Falls
Fishing Harbour fresh fish and crayfish from the Fisherman's Co-Op
Historical Museum also known as the Old Cable Station Museum, includes local history and that of shipping

Maits Rest 40 minute walk through magnificent rainforest
Marriners Lookout panoramic views of the coast and bay
Music Festival during March (mainly jazz)
Otway National Park
Paradise Picnic Reserve and Barham Fernery
Turtons Track famous forest drive between Haines Junction and Beech Forest

Population....................................1200	Art Gallery	Museum	Airfield	Post Office
Distance from Melbourne (km)...187	Boat Charter	Picnic Ground	Autogas	RACV
Hotels...2	Bushwalking	Playground	Bank	SLSC Patrols
Motels...10	Craft Shop	Safe Swimming-	Boat Ramp	Supermarket
Caravan Parks....................................5	Diving	beach	Churches (3)	Take Away Food
Cottages / Bed & Breakfast............10	Golf Course	Saturday Market	EFTPOS	Toilets
Flats & Units 90	Gymnasium	Scenic Flights	Hospital	Tourist Info.
Guest House 1	Historical Society	Surfing	Medical Centre	
Hostel / Backpackers........................1	Horse Trail Rides	Swimming Pool	Newsagent	
Host Farms...2	Jetty	Tea-rooms	Petrol Station	
Restaurants 5	Lawn Bowls	Tennis Courts	Police Station	

BLANKET BAY

Historically, Blanket Bay served as the safe landing point for provisions to the Cape Otway lighthouse. The supply vessels were displaced by railway and bullock wagons in the early 1900s. Today, Blanket Bay is one of six camping grounds in the Otway National Park. It is a bit of a trek getting there, but well worth the effort. There are only sixteen camp sites (plus an area set aside for hikers), so if you find the camp full there is always the next national park site at Aire River, some twenty minutes away (sites cannot be booked). Blanket Bay is amazingly protected from the westerly weather, wonderfully isolated and exceptionally beautiful. There are sandy beaches with reefs for fossicking and endless rock pools for inquisitive young minds. It's a sensational spot to camp or just visit for the day. Take your own water, as it is otherwise only available from local creeks and rivers.

Bushwalking, Diving, Horse Trail Rides nearby, National Park, Picnic Ground, Safe Swimming Beach, Boat Ramp, Toilets

CAPE OTWAY

Located at the southernmost point along the Great Ocean Road, Cape Otway is a maritime reserve best known for its historic lighthouse, completed in 1848, making it the second oldest lighthouse in Australia. Cape Otway and King Island, ninety kilometres away, mark the western entrance to Bass Strait and its perilous reefs. During the early 1800s many ships were wrecked in the vicinity, with the loss of hundreds of lives. This prompted construction of the lighthouse in 1846, no easy feat considering the area was still unexplored. On the reserve and still occupied are the original light-keeper's quarters and an operating weather-station. There is also the old telegraph station, unfortunately now derelict. Indeed, the lighthouse has been redundant since January 1994 when a solar-powered beacon took over, but at least visitors are now permitted to ascend the lighthouse tower.

Accom. on the reserve, Bushwalking, B'packers & Caravan Park nearby, Lighthouse tours 052 379 240, National Park, Toilets

GLENAIRE

At Hordern Vale, the Great Ocean Road descends to the broad river plains of the Aire Valley. The road skirts around the flats at the base of the foothills then briefly rejoins the coast at Castle Cove, where there is a sandy, cliff-lined beach. Nestled behind the cove is Glenaire, where ruins of the Glen Aire Station homestead still remain from a farming settlement established in the 1840s. To the east, a short drive along a dirt road brings you to the Aire River and a series of small lakes. There are two Otway National Park camping grounds, on either side of the river, and a magnificent beach is a twenty minute walk away, alongside the cliff-lined estuary. It's definitely not for swimming though, as is the case all along this very exposed stretch of coastline between Cape Otway and Port Campbell. However, bathing in the river near the jetty is safe and Lake Craven is perfect for canoeing.

Accommodation (cabins and cottages), Bushwalking, Diving, National Park, Picnic Ground, River Jetty, Surfing, Toilets

JOHANNA

Johanna is essentially a dairy-farming area that came into the limelight in 1970 when the World Surfing Championships were moved from a very flat Bells Beach to perfect conditions at Johanna. The beach is huge and dramatic, with cliffs at either end and sand dunes in between. There are two car-parks, both right at the beach, and the second one doubles as a camping ground. It is fairly exposed and once again within the Otway National Park. Just two and a half kilometres inland along Blue Johanna Road is the Johanna Scenic Reserve with the Johanna Falls, and nearby but outside the reserve on private land are the Wangerrip Falls. Johanna's other interesting distinction is its proximity to Dinosaur Cove, where ongoing excavations by the Museum of Victoria have uncovered significant fossilized dinosaur bones over 100 million years old. It is not a safe swimming beach.

Accommodation (cottages & host farms), Bushwalking, Diving, National Park, Picnic Ground, Surfing, Tennis Courts, Toilets

LAVERS HILL

Lavers Hill is the only town described in this book that is not actually on the coast, but at the cross-roads of the Great Ocean Road. Straddling a ridge high up in the Otways, it has an average rainfall of over 2000 millimetres (that's nearly seven feet, so bring the gumboots), and not surprisingly the surrounding rainforest has mountain ash trees growing as high as one hundred metres. The town primarily serves the local farming community, whereas its early history evolved around logging and saw-milling. The native forests are still selectively logged today, but milled elsewhere, as is the case for the pine plantations. Nearby is Melba Gully State Park, once the site of popular tea-rooms operating during the 1930s and 1940s, now a beautiful picnic spot and forest walk famous for its glow-worms. Triplet Falls are to the east of Lavers Hill, easily accessible and quite sensational.

Art Gallery, Bushwalking, Craft Shop, Picnic Ground, Playground, Swimming Pool, Tea-rooms, Tennis Courts, Bank agency
B&B, Caravan Park, Church, General Store, Motel, Newsagent, Petrol, Post Office, Take Away Food, Toilets, Tourist Info

MOONLIGHT HEAD

Moonlight Head is five minutes down a winding road through beautiful bush (the turnoff is well signposted on the Great Ocean Road). It is at the western end of the Otway Ranges, but at the start of a magnificent stretch of coastal cliffs. In fact, with sheer drops of 130 metres they are reputed to be the highest sea-cliffs in Australia. There are two walks, a short one through a dense copse of sheoaks to the Gable Lookout and a second track going right down to Wreck Beach, where the anchors from the shipwrecks *Marie Gabrielle* and *Fiji* lie embedded in rocks. There are 350 steps to the beach, so be prepared. Semi-precious gemstones are commonly found on beaches in the area, but getting to them is another question. Camping is not permitted, so really it is a place to day-visit only, to explore isolated beaches and tracks, perfect for the fit and curious.

Bushwalking, Diving, Gemstoning, Horse Trail Rides, Moonlight Head Cemetery, National Park, Surfing

PRINCETOWN

Having departed from the coast since Apollo Bay, the Great Ocean Road returns to the sea at Princetown. It's a tiny township, comprising an archetypal country general-store, perched atop a small hill. Scattered about are a handful of impromptu houses, whilst below snakes the Gellibrand River and its flood-plain rich in birdlife. Downstream is the prominent headland of Point Ronald and its sensational limestone cliffs defining the estuary on one side, and generous sand dunes on the other. It makes for an exhilarating walk to the beach, and although exposed and unsafe for swimming it is well worth the effort. (There is safe swimming in the estuary.) Further afield are Clifton and Rivernook Beaches, perfect for the more adventurous type, or ocean fishermen who like remote spots. Just before the turnoff to the township is the Old Ocean Road. It crosses the flats then winds through a beautiful valley beside the Gellibrand River until it meets the Great Ocean Road at Lower Gellibrand. Princetown has the honour of bounding both the Otway and Port Campbell National Parks.

ATTRACTIONS
Birdlife on the Gellibrand River flood-plain and estuary
Clifton Beach and Rivernook Beach
Gibson Steps dramatic beach via steps cut into cliff-face
Glenample Homestead and historic displays

Old Coach Road sandy track to Moonlight Head
Otway & Port Campbell National Parks
Otway Ranges Deer & Wildlife Park 8 km east of P'town
The Twelve Apostles uniquely famous array of island rock stacks (Fairy Penguins return at dusk)

Population.....................................20	
Distance from Melbourne (km)...273	
Hotel...-	
Motel..-	
Caravan Parks...................................2	
Cottages / Bed & Breakfast..............6	
Flats & Units....................................-	
Guest House......................................-	
Hostel / Backpackers........................1	
Host Farms..3	
Restaurant...-	

Bushwalking	General Store
Canoeing	Newsagent
Diving	Petrol
Helicopter Flights	Post Office
Horse Trail Rides	Take Away Food
National Parks	Toilets
Picnic Ground	
Surfing	
Tennis Courts	
Wildlife Park	
Boat Ramp	

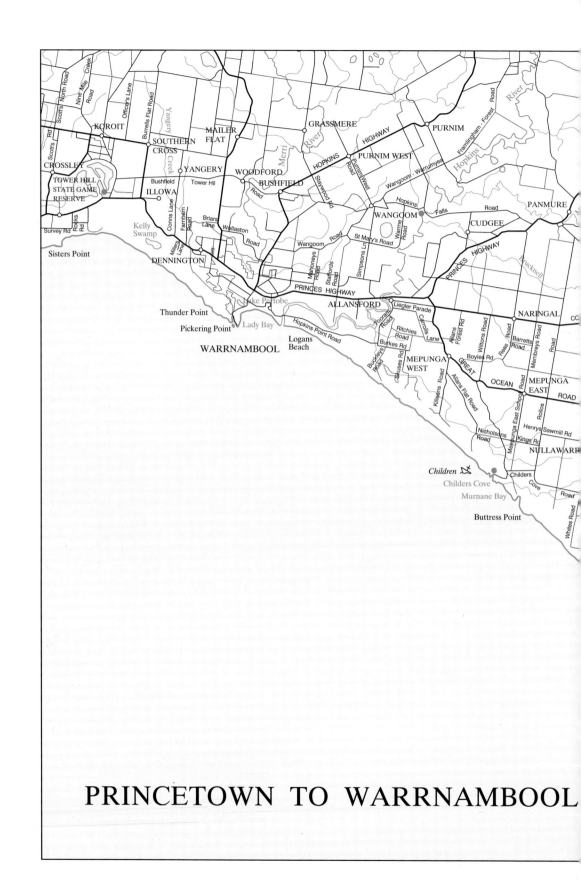

PRINCETOWN TO WARRNAMBOOL

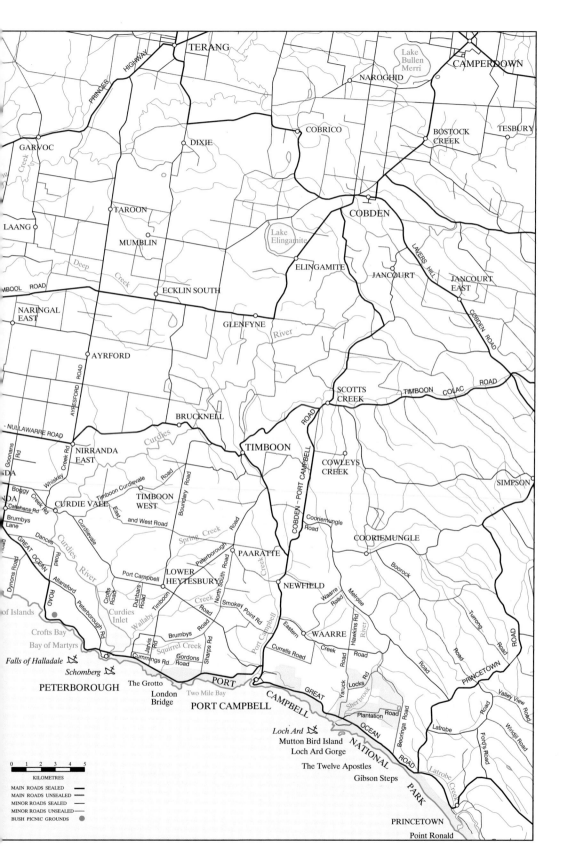

TERANG

CAMPERDOWN

Lake
Bullen
Merri

NAROGHID

COBRICO

BOSTOCK
CREEK

TESBURY

GARVOC

DIXIE

PRINCES HIGHWAY

Creek

TAROON

COBDEN

LAANG

MUMBLIN

Lake
Elingamite

ELINGAMITE

JANCOURT

JANCOURT
EAST

Deep

Creek

ECKLIN SOUTH

MBOOL ROAD

LAVERS HILL

COBDEN ROAD

NARINGAL
EAST

GLENFYNE

River

AYRFORD

AYRESFORD ROAD

SCOTTS
CREEK

TIMBOON COLAC ROAD

BRUCKNELL

ROAD

NULLAWARRE ROAD

Curdies

TIMBOON

COWLEYS
CREEK

SIMPSON

Goonans Rd

NIRRANDA
EAST

Whiskey Creek Rd

Creek Rd

Road

COBDEN — PORT CAMPBELL ROAD

DA

Boggy

Callahans Rd

Creek Rd

CURDIE VALE

Timboon Curdievale

TIMBOON
WEST

Boundary Road

Cooriemungle
Road

COORIEMUNGLE

NDA

Brumbys
Lane

Curdievale

East

and West Road

Spring Creek

Road

Boorock

GREAT OCEAN

Dances

Curdies River

Road

PEERBOROUGH Rd

Allansford

Peterborough Road

Port Campbell

LOWER
HEYTESBURY

PAARATTE

Creek

Melrose

Dynons Road

ROAD

Crofts Road

Dunbars
Road

North South Road

NEWFIELD

Waarre
Road

Hawkins Rd

of Islands

Curdies
Inlet

Timboon

Smokey Point Rd

WAARRE

Turrong Road

Crofts Bay
Bay of Martyrs

Wallaby

Brumbys

Sharps Rd

Road

Eastern

Creek

Road

Road

PRINCETOWN ROAD

Falls of Halladale

Squirrel Creek

Road

Currells Road

Valley View Road

Schomberg

Cummings Rd

Gordons
Road

Port Campbell

PORT

Yaruck

Locks Rd

Road

Latrobe

Ford's Road

PETERBOROUGH

The Grotto

London
Bridge

Two Mile Bay

CAMPBELL

GREAT

Locks

Sherbrook

Booringa Road

Windjill Road

PORT CAMPBELL

Plantation

Road

OCEAN

Loch Ard

Mutton Bird Island
Loch Ard Gorge

NATIONAL

ROAD

Latrobe

The Twelve Apostles

Gibson Steps

PARK

Creek

PRINCETOWN

Point Ronald

0 1 2 3 4 5
KILOMETRES

MAIN ROADS SEALED
MAIN ROADS UNSEALED
MINOR ROADS SEALED
MINOR ROADS UNSEALED
BUSH PICNIC GROUNDS

PORT CAMPBELL

Port Campbell is another jewel in the Great Ocean Road's crown, albeit a rough diamond. It is located beside the Norfolk pine-lined inlet of Port Campbell Bay, with its safe and protected beach. A sizeable jetty is the launching place for the local crayfishing fleet and on the opposite side of the bay a discovery walk follows the cliff edge to Two Mile Bay. Surrounding the inlet are rugged limestone cliffs, etched by the elements into magnificent forms, in particular, the Twelve Apostles for which the Port Campbell National Park is so famous. Indeed, it must have one of the greatest collections of coastal wonders in the world. Extensive boardwalks and steps cater for sightseeing at the main attractions in the park, but there is also the odd fishing track with magical surprises. This jagged coastline has claimed many shipwrecks, the most famous being that of the *Loch Ard* in 1878. But not even the cliffs, into which these vessels were often driven, can defy the ravages of the sea, for in 1990 a section of London Bridge collapsed, stranding two tourists temporarily. So beware.

ATTRACTIONS

Historical Society

Jetty and crane for lifting boats

Loch Ard Gorge convoluted part of the coastline with caves, gorges and blowhole

Loch Ard Shipwreck Museum

London Bridge famous sea-cliff arch

Mutton Bird Island birds return at dusk between September and May

Port Campbell National Park and Information Centre including natural history displays

Port Campbell Beach picturesque and safe beach

The Twelve Apostles uniquely famous formation of island rock stacks (Fairy Penguins return at dusk)

The Arch unusual sea-cliff formation

Timboon Farmhouse Cheese biodynamic cheeses

Two Mile Bay via the Great Ocean Road or discovery walk along the cliffs of Port Campbell Bay

Population.....................................200	Art Gallery	Playground	EFTPOS
Distance from Melbourne (km)...292	Boat Charter	Safe Swimming-	General Store
Hotel...1	Bushwalking	beach	Newsagent
Motels..4	Craft Shop	Sunday Market	Petrol Station
Caravan Park 1	Diving	Surfing	Police Station
Cottages / Bed & Breakfast..............3	Helicopter Flights	Tea-rooms	Post Office
Flats & Units....................................-	Historical Society	Tennis Courts	RACV
Guest House......................................-	Jetty	Autogas	SLSC Patrols
Hostel / Backpackers........................1	Museum	Bank (agency)	Take Away Food
Host Farms.......................................4	National Park	Boat Ramp	Toilets
Restaurants 2	Picnic Ground	Church	Tourist Info.

PETERBOROUGH

The seascape flattens out at Peterborough, which is positioned at the mouth of the massive Curdies Inlet. Black swans, in large numbers, seem always to be in residence. On one side of the estuary are large sand dunes and an exposed beach, whilst on the other there is a return to low sandstone cliffs carved into a complex pattern of coves and secluded beaches. By and large these are safe for swimming on calm days, and there is always the estuary. Two hundred metres or so offshore and just east of the rivermouth is Schomberg Reef. It is hard to believe, but on a calm, moonlit night in 1855 one of the largest and most luxurious clippers of the period ran aground here on her maiden voyage. No lives were lost, but the reputation of the Schomberg's captain, "Bully" Forbes, was certainly lost from then on. Peterborough is a popular haven for Victoria's western-district farmers, many of whom frequent the Peterborough Golf Club. This golf course is a piece of magic for golfers of all abilities, given its forgiving nature and despite being located, at times, a bit too close to the ocean.

ATTRACTIONS

Bay of Islands Coastal Park picturesque group of small rocky islands

Bay of Martyrs and Crofts Bay adjoining bays with clusters of small rock stacks

Curdies Inlet and abundant birdlife

Massacre Bay rugged surfing and fishing location

Peterborough Golf Links par three, nine hole course with panoramic views of the coast

Ralph Illidge Sanctuary birdlife 25 km north of P'borough

Secluded Beaches amongst the sheltered coves

The Grotto unusual sea-cliff formation

Population.....................................250	Bushwalking	Swimming Pool
Distance from Melbourne (km)...305	Canoeing	Tennis Courts
Hotel...1	Diving	Airfield
Motels..2	Golf Course	Boat Ramps
Caravan Parks...................................2	National Park	General Store
Cottages / Bed & Breakfast.............-	Picnic Ground	Newsagent
Flats & Units....................................-	Playground	Petrol
Guest House.....................................-	Safe Swimming-	Post Office
Hostel / Backpackers........................-	beach	Take Away Food
Host Farm ....-	Scenic Flights	Toilets
Restaurant..1	Surfing	

CHILDERS COVE

Named after the wreck of the coastal trader *Children* in 1839, Childers Cove is only a five-minute detour from the main road but seems a lot more remote. Surrounded by pasture there are three adjoining bays: Sandy Bay, Murnanes Bay and Childers Cove. By and large this is the only accessible part of the coast between the Bay of Islands and Warrnambool, a stretch of some thirty kilometres. The terrain has changed once again since the Bay of Islands, though there are still some cliffs and a smattering of rocky islands or "stacks". Childers Cove and Murnanes Bay both have protected beaches, safe for swimming if the swell is not too large, and both are accessible by way of elaborate zig-zagging steps. These are very much in keeping with a tradition of inspired wooden structures for access and viewing all the way along the Great Ocean Road. Camping is prohibited.

Bushwalking, Diving, Picnic Ground, Toilets

WARRNAMBOOL

Warrnambool's diverse range of commercial, cultural and historical facilities makes it a sophisticated city, though with a strong coastal flavour that is most engaging. It is the largest town on the Great Ocean Road and a significant trading centre servicing, a good deal of Victoria's western dfistrict farms. An impressive avenue of Norfolk pines creates a graceful entrance along the Princes Highway, with glimpses of the ocean not far away. Lady Bay provides the focus for many recreational and tourist attractions, including protected beaches and the extensive Flagstaff Hill Maritime Museum which overlooks it. Most apt, considering about twenty ships lie wrecked in the bay. A kilometre to the east of the Hopkins Rivermouth is Logans Beach, famous as a whale nursery. Every May, female southern right whales come here to calve, and they can be easily seen close to the shore over several months before they depart in October for their Antarctic summer feeding grounds.

ATTRACTIONS

Allansford Cheeseworld at Kraft's factory east of W'bool
Art Gallery and Performing Arts Centre
Botanic Gardens
Flagstaff Hill Maritime Museum recreation of early Australian port and village
History House Warrnambool Historical Society exhibits
Hopkins Falls eels migrate up the falls in early Summer
Hopkins Rivermouth
Lake Pertobe Adventure Playground

Southern Right Whales at Logans Beach
Thunder Point Coastal Reserve and Fairy Penguin colony on Middle Island
Time & Tide Museum collection of shells, clocks and musical instruments
Tower Hill State Game Reserve 13 km west of Warrnambool
Warrnambool Aquarium and Marine Museum
Warrnambool May Racing Carnival & Annual Steeplechase
Wunta Festival four days of celebrations, exhibitions and events in late February

Population25,500	Art Gallery	Museum	Tennis Courts	Petrol Station
Distance from Melbourne (km)...358	Aquarium	Picnic Ground	Airfield	Police Station
Hotels10	Bushwalking	Playground	Autogas	Post Office
Motels23	Craft Shop	Safe Swimming-	ATM	RACV
Caravan Parks8	Diving	beach	Bank	SLSC Patrols
Cottages / Bed & Breakfast8	Golf Course	Scenic Flights	Boat Ramp	Supermarket
Flats & Units130	Gymnasium	Squash Courts	Churches (19)	Take Away Food
Guest Houses2	Historical Society	Sunday Market	EFTPOS	Toilets
Hostel / Backpackers1	Horse Trail Rides	Surfing	Hospital	Tourist Info.
Host Farms3	Jetty	Swimming Pool	Medical Centre	
Restaurants22	Lawn Bowls	Tea-rooms	Newsagent	

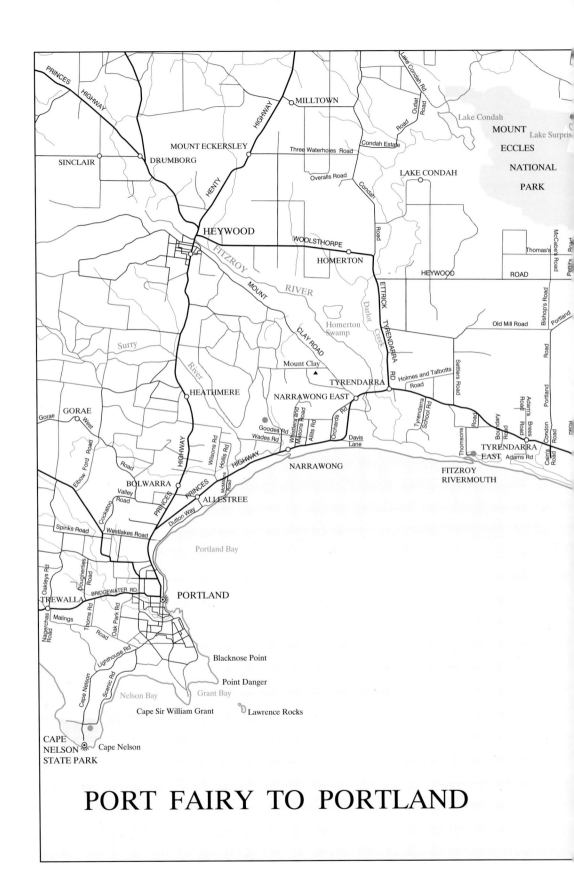

PORT FAIRY TO PORTLAND

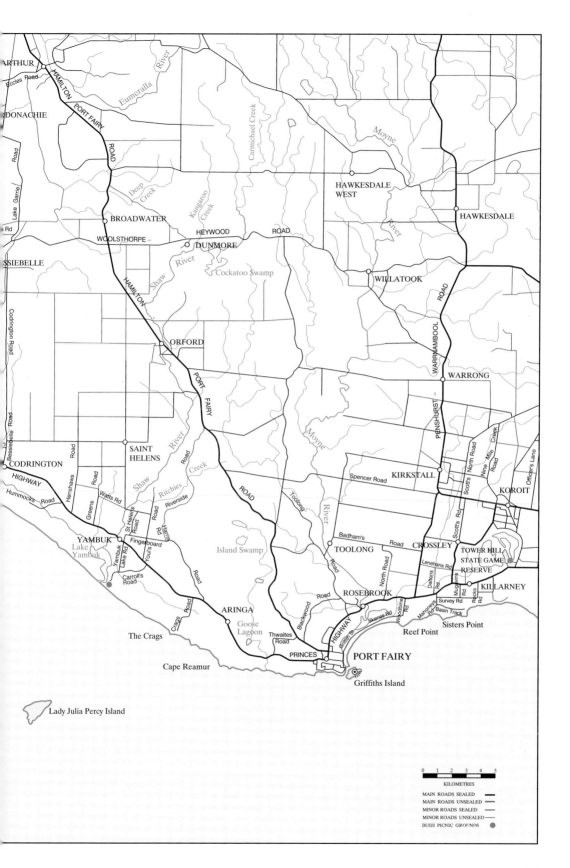

ARTHUR

Eccles Road

HAMILTON PORT FAIRY ROAD

DONACHIE

Eumeralla River

Carmichael Creek

Moyne

Road

Lake Garrie

Rd

Codrington Road

Deep Creek

Kangaroo Creek

River

HAWKESDALE WEST

HAWKESDALE

BROADWATER

WOOLSTHORPE

HEYWOOD ROAD

DUNMORE

Shaw River

Cockatoo Swamp

WILLATOOK

SSIEBELLE

HAMILTON

WARRNAMBOOL ROAD

ORFORD

PORT FAIRY

Bessiebelle Road

PENSHURST

SAINT HELENS

WARRONG

Shaw River

Ritchies Creek

HIGHWAY

Henshaws Road

Greens Road

Watts Rd

Road

Riverside Road

Harris Rd

ROAD

Toolong River

Spencer Road

KIRKSTALL

Scotts North Road

Nine Mile Creek

Officer's Lane

KOROIT

Hummocks Road

St Helen's Road

Fingerboard

Your's Rd

Badham's Road

TOOLONG

Road

North Road

CROSSLEY

Scotts Rd

Scotts Rd

Moyne

YAMBUK

Lake Yambuk

Yambuk Lake Rd

Island Swamp

Lenehans Rd

TOWER HILL STATE GAME RESERVE

Carroll's Road

Road

Road

ROSEBROOK

Daltons Rd

Mugleys Rd

Ricks Rd

KILLARNEY

ARINGA

Goose Lagoon

Blackwood Road

HIGHWAY

Griffith St

Skenes Rd

Woodbine Rd

Mahoneys Rd

Survey Rd

Basin Track

Sisters Point

The Crags

Craigs Road

Thwaites Road

PRINCES

Reef Point

Cape Reamur

PORT FAIRY

Griffiths Island

Lady Julia Percy Island

0 1 2 3 4 5
KILOMETRES

MAIN ROADS SEALED
MAIN ROADS UNSEALED
MINOR ROADS SEALED
MINOR ROADS UNSEALED
BUSH PICNIC GROUNDS

KILLARNEY

In the midst of potato and onion fields, Killarney is only a small settlement but manages to extend itself some distance along the highway. A kilometre or two in the distance can be seen a low continuous sand dune that defines the coastline between Warrnambool and Port Fairy. Killarney Beach, where the camping ground is located, provides for safe swimming as a result of a string of exposed reefs blocking out the swell. They also attract a great number of water birds. Somewhere in the sand dunes along this part of the coast lies the mysterious Mahogany Ship, speculated to be a Portuguese caravel lost in the early 1500s. Wreckage was last sighted in the 1880s. The remains are presumed to be buried under drifting dunes, though extensive searches have failed to locate them. Just to the east of Killarney is the Tower Hill State Game Reserve, an extinct volcano now noted for its wildlife, especially the freely roaming emus always thrusting their agile necks in the direction of anything that looks like food. A natural history centre provides elaborate displays and information.

ATTRACTIONS
Birdlife and Reefs
Protected Beach
The Mahogany Walking Track between Warrnambool and Port Fairy
Tower Hill State Game Reserve bushwalks and wildlife and lake within a volcanic crater

Population	150	Bushwalking	General Store
Distance from Melbourne (km)	374	Diving	Newsagent
Hotel	1	Picnic Ground	Petrol
Motel	-	Playground	Take Away Food
Caravan Park	1	Safe Swimming-	Toilets
Cottages / Bed & Breakfast	1	beach	
Flats & Units	-	State Park	
Guest House	-	Tennis Courts	
Hostel / Backpackers	-	Wildlife Park	
Host Farm	1	Boat Ramp	
Restaurant	-	Church	

PORT FAIRY

Steeped in history and charm, Port Fairy is located at the mouth of the Moyne River which provides a natural harbour, flurried with yachts and fishing boats. The hunting of whales and seals in the past has given way to crayfish and abalone fishing, most appropriate for such a hospitable town with a reputation for cottage and bed-and-breakfast accommodation. Hunting of the southern right whale came to a close in the early 1840s when their supply was all but exhausted. Two Irish land developers, James Atkinson and William Rutledge, revived the town in the mid 1840s and named it Belfast. Fellow Irish folk needed little encouragement to emigrate and escape the Irish potato famine, thereby establishing potato farming in the area. As in so many towns along the Great Ocean Road, avenues of Norfolk pines are common and most striking alongside the harbour. Each Labour Day weekend in March, Port Fairy hosts Australia's largest folk music festival, and the Spring Music Festival in October is growing in reputation as a classical music event.

ATTRACTIONS
Battery Hill fortifications, including cannons and lookout
Boat Harbour on the Moyne River
Cafe Gazette Museum sporting memorabilia
Folk Music Festival during Labour Day weekend
Griffiths Island Lighthouse
Historic Buildings over 50 classified by the National Trust
Motts Cottage restored stone cottage and historic displays

Mount Eccles National Park lake in the volcanic craters
Muttonbird Colony on Griffiths Island, nesting between September and May
Port Fairy Aquarium & Shark Pool
Port Fairy Historic Lifeboat Station rocket house and lifeboat shed used for shipwreck rescues
Port Fairy Historical Society Museum
The Crags cliff area and diving spot 12 km west of Port Fairy

Population.................................2,600	Aquarium	Museum	Bank	Supermarket
Distance from Melbourne (km)...387	Art Gallery	Picnic Ground	Boat Ramp	Take Away Food
Hotels 4	Boat Charter	Playground	Churches (5)	Toilets
Motels.................................7	Bushwalking	Safe Swimming-	EFTPOS	Tourist Info.
Caravan Parks.................................6	Craft Shop	beach	Medical Centre	
Cottages / Bed & Breakfast............20	Diving	Squash Courts	Newsagent	
Flats & Units 45	Golf Course	Surfing	Petrol Station	
Guest House 1	Historical Society	Tea-rooms	Police Station	
Hostel / Backpackers.......................1	River Jetty	Tennis Courts	Post Office	
Host Farm 1	Lawn Bowls	Airfield	RACV	
Restaurants 6	Lighthouse	Autogas	SLSC Patrols	

YAMBUK

The main Yambuk township is on the Princes Highway, but four kilometres south, beside Lake Yambuk, is a smaller outpost that has captured all the charm. Below the holiday houses and beside the camping ground, the lake narrows, winding through a landscape of impressive sand dunes on its way to the sea. It is an unusual but splendid vista, and all the more interesting for the plateau-like form of Lady Julia Percy Island eight kilometres offshore, with its seal colony numbering over four thousand. Surrounded by almost vertical cliffs between thirty and forty-five metres high, this island of volcanic origins is home to blue penguins, mutton birds, kestrels and swamp harriers. Lake Yambuk also abounds with birdlife of all descriptions, including the intriguing small "divers" and those fanciful feeders, pelicans. The lake is the safest spot for swimming, rather than the current-swept ocean. Five kilometres to the east of Yambuk are the Crags, an elevated cliff with rocky foreshore below, making a popular diving spot in calm seas.

ATTRACTIONS
Lady Julia Percy Island sea-birds and seal colony
Lake Condah Aboriginal Mission Site to the west of
Mount Eccles National Park
Lake Yambuk for fishing, boating and birdlife
Long Slide in the sand dunes, one hundred feet long
Mount Eccles National Park lake in the volcanic craters

Population	250	Bushwalking	General Store
Distance from Melbourne (km)	404	Canoeing	Newsagent
Hotel	1	Diving	Petrol
Motel	-	River Jetty	Post Office
Caravan Park	1	Picnic Ground	Take Away Food
Cottages / Bed & Breakfast	1	Playground	Toilets
Flats & Units	-	Surfing	
Guest House	-	Tennis Courts	
Hostel / Backpackers	-	Bank (agency)	
Host Farm	-	Boat Ramp	
Restaurant	-	Churches (2)	

FITZROY RIVERMOUTH

If you really want to get away from it all and get back to basics, then the Fitzroy Rivermouth is just the place for those of ascetic inclinations. The turnoff, easily missed, is twenty-two kilometres west of Yambuk along the Princes Highway. A short drive brings you to the Fitzroy River where it runs parallel and close to the ocean beach before turning into the sea. At this point there is a camping and picnic ground, though facilities are basic (pit toilets and no water). Once again, along this stretch of coastline the river provides for safe swimming rather than the ocean. A jetty and boat ramp into the river caters for fishermen with small boats. The western district of Victoria has a rich Aboriginal heritage, since many clans once lived in the area. Near Mount Eccles National Park is the site of the Lake Condah Aboriginal Mission, now in ruins. Perhaps of more interest though, are the ancient fish-traps and remains of stone houses constructed by the Aborigines thousands of years ago.

Bushwalking, B&B (nearby), Boat Ramp, Canoeing, Diving, Mount Eccles National Park, Picnic Ground, River Jetty

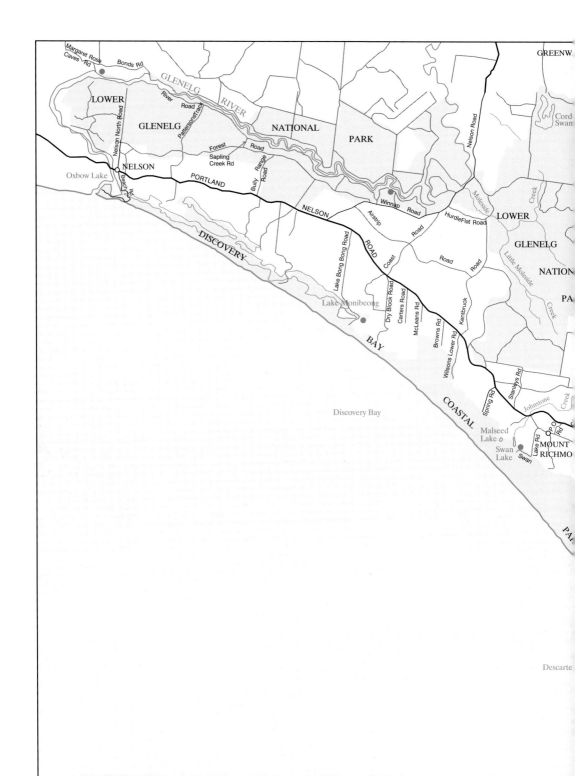

PORTLAND TO NELSON

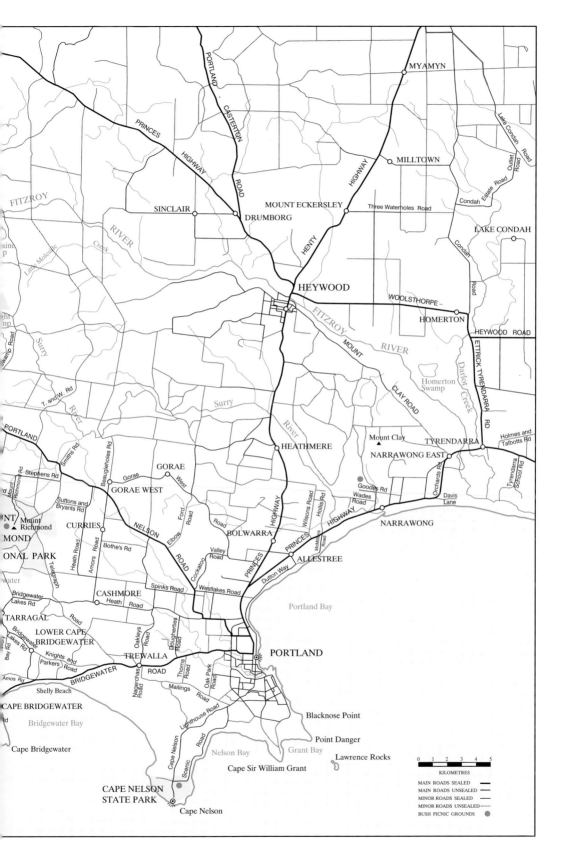

MYAMYN

PORTLAND CASTERTON ROAD

PRINCES HIGHWAY

HIGHWAY

MILLTOWN

FITZROY

RIVER

Little Molleste Creek

SINCLAIR

DRUMBORG

MOUNT ECKERSLEY

Three Waterholes Road

LAKE CONDAH

Lake Condah Road

Outlet Road

Condah Estate Road

HENTY

HEYWOOD

WOOLSTHORPE

HOMERTON

HEYWOOD ROAD

Condah Road

FITZROY MOUNT RIVER

Surry

Swamp Road

T. and W. Rd

Surry

River

Homerton Swamp

Darlot Creek

ETTRICK TYRENDARRA RD

PORTLAND

HEATHMERE

Mount Clay

CLAY ROAD

Holmes and Talbotts Rd

Smiths Rd

Stephens Rd

GORAE

GORAE WEST

Gorae West

Ford Road

Road

Beaugleholes Rd

HIGHWAY

Wilsons Road

Hollis Rd

Goodes Rd

Wades Road

NARRAWONG EAST

TYRENDARRA

Orchards Rd

Davis Lane

Tyrendarra School Rd

Mount Richmond Rd

Suttons and Bryants Rd

CURRIES

NELSON

Bothe's Rd

BOLWARRA

Elbow Road

Valley Road

PRINCES

HIGHWAY

McMahons Road

NARRAWONG

NT

Mount Richmond

MOND

ONAL PARK

water

ROAD

Amors Road

Cockatoo

ALLESTREE

Heath Road

Telegraph

Spinks Road

Westlakes Road

Dutton Way

CASHMORE

Heath Road

Portland Bay

Bridgewater Lakes Rd

TARRAGAL

LOWER CAPE BRIDGEWATER

Road

Oakleys Road

Dougherties Road

Bay Rd

Bridgewater Lakes Rd

Knights and Parkers Road

TREWALLA

ROAD

Thorns Road

Oak Park Road

PORTLAND

Amos Rd

BRIDGEWATER

Nagerchas Road

Mailings Road

CAPE BRIDGEWATER

Shelly Beach

Rd

Bridgewater Bay

Cape Bridgewater

Lighthouse Road

Cape Nelson Scenic Road

Nelson Bay

Grant Bay

Blacknose Point

Point Danger

Lawrence Rocks

Cape Sir William Grant

CAPE NELSON STATE PARK

Cape Nelson

0 1 2 3 4 5
KILOMETRES

MAIN ROADS SEALED ▬▬
MAIN ROADS UNSEALED ▬▬
MINOR ROADS SEALED ───
MINOR ROADS UNSEALED ───
BUSH PICNIC GROUNDS ●

43

NARRAWONG

Just before Narrawong the Princes Highway rejoins the ocean. The Narrawong Camping and Recreational Reserve tends to dominate the foreshore and is almost encircled by the Surry River (spelt without an 'e' despite the road authorities' efforts to include it). It is an extremely popular camping spot during summer, with safe swimming and canoeing in the river that is often sand-barred from the sea. The ocean beach (mostly safe for swimming) is endless, stretching all the way to Portland, visible in the distance. Just behind Narrawong is the Sawpit Picnic Ground, named for the hole in the ground used last century for hand-sawing logs. Close by is Whalers Lookout, providing excellent ocean views and the possibility of seeing a whale if binoculars and luck are with you. In the Narrawong cemetery lies the grave of Captain William Dutton, a sealer whom locals claim to be the first true settler of the area in the early 1830s, rather than the Hentys of Portland, though it is conceded that they were the first to develop the land.

ATTRACTIONS
Camping and Recreation Reserve
Narrawong State Forest half of which is a flora and fauna reserve protecting heathland

Mount Eccles National Park lake in volcanic craters
Sawpit Picnic Ground and Whalers Lookout
Lake Condah Aboriginal Mission Site to the west of Mount Eccles National Park

Population.....................................180	Bushwalking	Post Office
Distance from Melbourne (km)...441	Canoeing	Take Away Food
Hotel...-	Diving	Toilets
Motel..-	Picnic Ground	
Caravan Park 1	Playground	
Cottages / Bed & Breakfast..............-	Surfing	
Flats & Units....................................-	Tennis Courts	
Guest House......................................-	Boat Ramp	
Hostel / Backpackers........................-	General Store	
Host Farm ....-	Newsagent	
Restaurant...-	Petrol	

PORTLAND

Though the area was frequented by sealers and whalers in the early 1800s, it was not until 1834 that Edward Henty first tilled the soil, thereby establishing Portland as the first European settlement in Victoria. The depth of history is conspicuous, with over 100 historic buildings. Of particular note are the Court House and Customs House, the latter being the oldest government building still in use in Australia. The city today revolves around its deep-water port and attendant industries, including sheep and meat export, crayfishing and aluminium smelting. It is especially noteworthy for its geo-thermal energy program, using naturally heated water from bores 1200 metres deep. Protected from the south-west weather by Cape Grant, Portland Bay offers calm-water beaches and a safe harbour with wharves that are accessible to the public. In 1859 the Portland lifeboat rescued survivors from the wreck of the steamship *Admella*. In 1989 fund-raising efforts to restore the lifeboat inspired a surf lifeboat race that has now grown into an annual festival, staged over a weekend in November.

ATTRACTIONS
Admella Surf Boat Marathon in November
Portland Aluminium Smelter guided tours (ph.Tourist Info)
Art Galleries
Battery Point historic defence installation including displays
Botanic Gardens and historic cottage including exhibits
Cape Nelson State Park and Cape Nelson Lighthouse
Fawthrop Lagoon flora & fauna wetland in the town centre
Fairy Penguin Colony at Henty Beach

Harbour and Wharves accessible to the public
History House local history museum
Lions Club Fauna Park native animals in natural parkland
Mount Eccles and Mount Richmond National Parks
Portland Regional Seed Bank landcare displays
Powerhouse Motor and Car Museum
Steam Packet Inn restored historic hotel
The Great South West Walk (see page 102)
The Place swimming pool and recreation complex

Population.................................12,000	Art Gallery	Lighthouse	Swimming Pool	Hospital
Distance from Melbourne (km)...458	Boat Charter	Museum	Tea-rooms	Medical Centre
Hotels 4	Bushwalking	National Parks	Tennis Courts	Newsagent
Motels...10	Craft Shop	Picnic Ground	Wildlife Park	Petrol Station
Caravan Parks..................................6	Diving	Playground	Airfield	Police Station
Cottages / Bed & Breakfast.............4	Golf Course	Safe Swimming-	Autogas	Post Office
Flats & Units 18	Gymnasium	beach	ATM	RACV
Guest Houses....................................2	Historical Society	Squash Courts	Bank	Supermarket
Hostel / Backpackers........................2	Horse Trail Rides	State Park	Boat Ramp	Take Away Food
Host Farms.......................................2	Jetty	Sunday Market	Churches (11)	Toilets
Restaurants 14	Lawn Bowls	Surfing	EFTPOS	Tourist Info.

CAPE BRIDGEWATER

The first sight one has of Cape Bridgewater is Stoney Hill, a massive, sheer cliff-face over 120 metres high. The cape was once a volcanic island, but is now connected to the mainland by sand dunes laid down over time, which eventually turned to limestone. The contrasting combination of limestone overlaying basalt cliffs is in evidence near the Petrified Forest at the end of the cape. Don't expect anything too lofty in the way of petrified monuments, nevertheless it's an intriguing and unusual spectacle. Nestled into the western end of Bridgewater Bay and not far from Stoney Hill is the small township of Cape Bridgewater. The surf life saving clubhouse, toilets, picnic ground and kiosk line up along a grassy foreshore above the beach, and that's about it as far as facilities are concerned. Above and dotted on the hillside are a cluster of houses, each with glorious panoramic views of Bridgewater Bay sweeping around to Cape Nelson, the lighthouse visible in the distance.

ATTRACTIONS
Blowholes creating spectacular spouts of spray in a big sea
Bridgewater Lakes for swimming, boating and fishing
Freshwater Springs water pools on coastal rock platforms

Mount Richmond National Park variety of bushwalks and lookout tower
Petrified Forest tree trunks thought to be transformed to sandstone (it is a theory now in question)

Population......................................60	
Distance from Melbourne (km)...480	
Hotel..-	
Motel...-	
Caravan Park....................................-	
Cottages / Bed & Breakfast.............2	
Flats & Units....................................-	
Guest House 1	
Hostel / Backpackers.......................-	
Host Farm ....-	
Restaurant.......................................-	

Bushwalking	SLSC Patrols
Diving	Take Away Food
Horse Trail Rides	Toilets
Picnic Ground	
Safe Swimming-beach	
Surfing	
Tennis Courts	
Boat Ramp	
General Store	
Newsagent	

NELSON

The road to Nelson is a narrow passageway through towering pine plantations and must be shared with kangaroos and emus, especially at dusk. The township is beside, if not in many respects actually on, the Glenelg River. And what a river! This is the stuff of boating and canoeing enthusiasts' watery dreams, a truly noble and impressive waterway that winds through bushland and limestone gorge, then widens into a shallow estuary just past Nelson. It is legendary for its fishing and prolific birdlife. River cruises, canoe and boat hire, even houseboat accommodation, are all available. The ocean can be reached by a short drive, then a walk beside the estuary. It is generally unsafe for swimming (whereas the estuary is fine), but worth a visit to take in the endless beach and sand dunes of Discovery Bay. These stretch virtually unbroken for fifty kilometres and form the Discovery Bay Coastal Park, whilst immediately to the north of Nelson is the Lower Glenelg National Park.

ATTRACTIONS

Discovery Bay Coastal Park and extensive sand-dunes
Estuary for fishing, safe swimming and birdlife
Glenelg River river cruises and canoeing

Lower Glenelg National Park and camping along the river
Piccaninnie Ponds diving in underwater limestone caverns
Princess Margaret Rose Caves with impressive stalactites and stalagmites

Population......................................200	Boat Charter	Tea Rooms	Toilets
Distance from Melbourne (km)...522	Bushwalking	Tennis Courts	Tourist Info.
Hotel..1	Canoeing	Airfield	
Motels..2	Diving	Bank (agency)	
Caravan Parks...................................2	Horse Trail Rides	Boat Ramps	
Cottages / Bed & Breakfast..............3	River Jetty	Church	
Flats & Units 1	National Park	General Store	
Guest House 1	Picnic Ground	Newsagent	
Hostel / Backpackers........................-	Playground	Petrol Station	
Host Farm ....-	State Park	Post Office	
Restaurant..-	Surfing	Take Away Food	

Above: Barwon Heads   Below: Queenscliff

DIARY OF A COASTAL WALK BY GEORGE ERNEST MORRISON

Born in 1862 and raised in Geelong, Ernest Morrison, at the age of 17 years undertook a walk from Queenscliff to Adelaide. Selected segments from his diary of the journey are reproduced below. A serialized version of it appeared in the Melbourne Leader during 1880, entitled "Diary of a Tramp". It marked the beginning of an illustrious career as journalist and traveller, and occaisional medical practitioner. His second legendary walk was during a break in medical studies in 1882. Taking 123 days, he journeyed over 3,000 kilometres from the Gulf of Carpenteria to Melbourne. Overseas travel and stints practising as a doctor followed, until in 1893 a trip to the Phillipines led him onto China, where he set about on yet another epic walk. He started at Shanghai, covering nearly 5,000 kilometres as he crossed China into Burma. Once again his account of the journey was published and ultimately resulted in his appointment as the first permanent correspondant in Asia for the London Times, based in Peking. He took up the post in 1897, remaining there for over 20 years, and became an expert in the politics of China. His contribution and influence was significant in the realms of international politics and earnt for him the title "Chinese Morrison".

Tuesday December 30, 1879: I left Queenscliff after an early lunch and it is my intention to endeavour to reach Bream Creek tonight, Swampy Creek tomorrow and then, by rising early and doing some hard walking, get into Lorne in time for my New Year's dinner. My attire was the subject of flattery as regards its usefulness, laughter as regards its appearance. On my head I wore a peaked hat which is certainly more suited for cold weather, but as it is so made that at will I could cover all my face with it except my eyes.

At Mama's earnest sollicitation I got a sun shade which fits on to the cap and protects the back of the head. My clothing consisted of a thick armless woollen guernsey, my cricketing shirt and cricketing coat, serge trousers specially strengthened, comfortable socks and a light but strong pair of boots. As a protection against snakes I also wore leggings.

On my back I carried a famous knapsack of my own invention. It was made of strong canvas doubled next back, but of a single piece outside and it had a partition down it. It was kept on my back by straps passing round my shoulders and round my waist and on the outside of it there were two straps intended for carrying my coat if it should be too hot to wear it.

My knapsack contained the following articles: two loaves of bread, a well roasted boneless leg of mutton; half a pound of salt, 1/4 lb. pepper; 3 lemons, two toothbrushes, a box of tooth powder, some rag, a towel, 5 pairs of socks, 2 cotton handkerchiefs, 2 silk, some soap and oilsilk. Writing materials and a comb; a small quotation and a note book. In the strap going round my waist was stuck a tomahawk. The only thing I carried was a billy with another one fitting inside it and this contained four penny boxes of matches, a box of zinc ointment, some twine, lead pencils, some flannel bandage and some calico. In one of my trouser pockets I carried a penknife, in the other my small chamois leather bag of money consisting of 3 £1 notes, two sovereigns, 10 half crowns, two shillings and 15 sixpences – altogether £6-14-6.

I was accompanied to the Barwon Heads by Harry Adams who had kindly volunteered to see me off. My knapsack was very heavy and hurt my back dreadfully. A fisherman put me across the river and I land at the Sheep Wash. I feel as I set off for Bream Creek [Breamlea] what an arduous walk I have undertaken, but with God's help I hope to get there all right. I am directed to a high sand cliff in the distance which I am told overlooks Bream Creek. I get there, but find it doesn't; there is another about a mile further on, perhaps that is it, again am I wrong, nothing daunted I make for a still more prominent hill, feeling sure that I must strike Bream Creek before I reach it, but alas disappointment again awaits me.

In despair I look around me. A road runs past a house in quite a different direction from where I am bound for, nevertheless I resolve to strike it. In doing so I have to cross a low marshy sort of plain covered with stunted bushes. I hear a rustling beside me and a large snake doesn't glide quick enough away to prevent me having a good look – a shuddering look at it. I get a glass of water at the house and am told if I follow up the road I am now on and take the second turning to the left, it will take me to the mouth of Bream Creek. At the first turning I was done up. It was about 9 o'clock. With my knapsack for a pillow I lie down on the bare ground in the corner of a paddock,

with a thorny hedge protecting me on two sides. The ground is prickly and cold. I try to get to sleep and commune with myself; O sleep, O gentle sleep – Nature's soft nurse, how have I frighted thee

> *That thou no more wilt weigh my eyelids down – And steep my senses in forgetfulness?*

Just as I am getting unconscious I am aroused by a fearful din seemingly at my ears. It is a number of boys at a house near; one or two are singing the Sweet by and bye, the rest keeping time with kerosene tins, bones, sticks and cetera. In turn we hear the following tunes or mutilations (variations) thereof: My grandfather's clock, Take it Bob, Hold the fort, Bonnie Dundee, God save the queen. If I'd a cow, and others. At length I go off into a sort of dreamy unconsciousness and though I was very cold and uncomfortable all night, when I woke in the morning I feel refreshed. I set off soon after daybreak for Bream Creek and walking there I had a glorious view of the sun rising. I don't think I ever saw a more magnificent sunrise, though it betokened a warm day.

Following the directions received overnight I soon found myself at the mouth of Bream Creek. This creek was running out and as it was two feet deep I had to take off my boots and stockings. Fishing off the rocks were two lads.

A pleasant walk of four miles along the hard sand brought me to two deserted fishermen's huts. From a well near I got excellent water. By taking a line cross country I saved two miles in getting to Spring Creek [Torquay]. No less than six tents were pitched in a bend of the river. Spring Creek, though larger than Bream, and just as salt, has its mouth always barred. High tide prevented me walking round the beach to Swampy Creek so I had to take to the cliffs. After having something to eat and boiling a billy of water I started. The cliffs here are magnificent. I have to walk along the edge and 300 ft below me the sea curled round the rock and dashed against its feet.....

I was much struck with the cliffs passed en route. Some would be rough and ragged, of a yellow colour, with

Above: Aireys Inlet Below: Anglesea golf course

Above and below: the Great Ocean Road between Lorne and Wye River
Next Page: Erskine Falls near Lorne

no trees near them; others perfectly perpendicular with the lines of formation horizontal, perpendicular or vertical. In other places cliff would rise above cliff, bare before me, but wooded on their summit, till they seemed almost to reach the sky.....When boiling my billy at Swampy Creek [Anglesea] two young residents in a house near came down to see me and their interest evinced itself more practically in the shape of a lent blanket, overcoat and pillow. My bed was in a clump of trees on the river's bank and lying awake with strange noises going on all round me I saw the Old Year 1879 out and the New Year 1880 in.

In the morning when I get up half an hour before sunrise, I find I am wet through; my boots and leggings especially are soaking. My feet also are raw and in no fit state do I feel for a long walk. From the top of the hill overlooking Swampy Creek I get a most glorious view. Away to the left stretched ranges of beautiful wooded hills and as the mist still hung over the valleys it looked as if a snowy lake nestled in snug places among the hills.

At the foot of the hill I am on, lies Swampy Creek placid in its smoothness and away beyond it I see the coast and cliffs extending miles upon miles. To my right lies the sea bank. Behind me tower still higher hills. I resolved instead of taking the ordinary road to Ayrey's Inlet through the ranges to try the old track which keeps near the coast.

I start and am led by the road a most delightful walk. The sea is in sight all the time and as the coast bends round a great deal I am enabled to distinguish Eaglehawk Peak and Loutitt Bay. The latter place gets more and more distinct till I can see the houses and fancy I distinguish the new hotel at the Point.....

Airey's Inlet is not a bay formed by the sea, though it may have been once. The inlet is a plain of low lying country covered with dead timber on one half, but cultivated in the half next the sea coast. Serpentining through it in a most extraordinary manner is Airey's Inlet Creek. A large gap in the coast hills has been made by nature to

Above, below and right: Apollo Bay

enable the river to enter the sea, but for reasons best known to itself it has failed to take advantage of this. I am very thirsty. It is now 8 a.m. There is a creek five miles round the beach. I hurry there, have a billy of tea, then going round a little further I take to the hills and follow the telegraph line over the tops of the hills. I again descend. A wash in the Reedy Creek and I start for Lorne which I reach by 3.30. Mount Joy's is very full. In the evening I go up to the Pacific Hotel to see Ted Nicholls. He shows me over it. It is magnificently furnished equal to anything I have ever seen. After New Year's dinner I resolved to sleep out. Mrs. Mountjoy lent me blanket, mattress

and pillow, Mr. Gerrard a water-proof. I spend an enjoyable night in the bathing house. Next morning after breakfast I start for Apollo Bay.

I had ordered a roast leg of mutton weighing 4 lbs. Judge of my disgust when a boiled leg, weighing nine pounds made its appearance. On my refusing it Mountjoy said there was only occasion to take enough for two meals as I could easily get to Apollo Bay that night. Accordingly I only took a couple of packets of sandwiches.

After tiresome jumping over rocks I arrive at the Cumberland, having passed the St. George and Sheoak. Arduous climbing for four miles took me to Jamieson's River, a creek very similar to the Cumberland and in a most picturesque situation. The whole of this stage was round the base of huge Mt. Defiance and I thought what a happy name it had. Another rest at the Jamieson and then a quiet walk, though hard on my sore feet, brought me to the Wye. This is a remarkably picturesque river, having, rising from its banks towering and splendidly wooded hills.

Saturday January 3rd: Here I found camped two men, Philip Henderson and Bob Straw, who had started from Lorne three hours before me. As it was very late in the day and I was very leg-weary I resolved to camp and go to Apollo Bay tomorrow with them, We fitted up a mia-mia, lit a glorious fire and I slept like a top; the others found it too cold. During the night we heard the lowing of wild bulls, the howling of wild dogs and the braying of native bears. We lit a glorious fire in front of our sleeping place and at 1.45 we got up, got warm and got back to bed again.

We started for Apollo Bay about half past seven. Four miles uninteresting walking over the hard but smooth rocks brought us to the Kennet, a fine large creek, but unfortunately salt and full of kelp. Henderson tried his hand at fishing, but unsuccessfully.....

We passed 13 creeks of fresh water and at each creek the scenery was more beautiful than at the others. The hills, though always very

similar in their appearance never tire the eye nor become monotonous. As we are walking along tired and noiselessly Henderson jumps back excitedly, calling 'A snake, there's a snake, I see a snake'. Mr. Straw did perhaps the fastest retrograde 25 yards ever seen, but he wasn't frightened, only alarmed. After a desperate and dangerous fight of half an hour with the snake we succeed in killing it. Its colour was something similar to the beach and I question if it wasn't harmless.

The name Apollo, though properly applied to the bay, has been transferred to the township, consisting of one house and a pigstye, it is situated on a grassy flat fronting the sea and protected by hills.....

Stopping at Cawood's are two gentlemen who are on an excursion something like mine, only a pleasure one. They are Kermot and Gregory, two celebrated men; the former a lecturer on Civil Engineering at the Melbourne University, the latter on Common Law. I had a glorious tea. My companions are going to stop here and tomorrow I shall go on with them as far as the Parker at least.

After many delays in saddling the pack horse etc., we set off. See us on the road: Mr. Gregory, a short broad-shouldered man with a long beard, slight stoop and handsome face, wearing a helmet hat; the very type of an explorer, leading. Myself in full war paint with bare arms next and Mr. Kernot, fairly tall, with a very round back, concave breast, narrow shoulders, knock knees, red nose and spectacles leading a packhorse. This horse is a perfect wonder of a traveller. He has climbed hills whereon the foot of horse has never before alighted, he has jumped over rocks never before seen by horse's eyes and what is more wonderful has turned somersaults down hill without hurting either himself or pack. These two travellers do not much believe in roughing it. In the pack which consists of four large bags of canvas they carry every luxury from a tent to lime juice, sweet biscuits and figs. Our route took an upward turn for miles and miles then into the ranges for miles and miles then out again for miles and miles and following along we came into sight of the sea at Blanket Bay. Previously to this on the top of a high hill I spied a snake. In deliberating in how we were to kill it, it slipped into a log and we were delayed half an hour getting it, much to Mr. Kernott's disgust. It was only by luck we did dislodge it after all. I could clearly see disappointment in the physiognomy of its countenance as it spat, jumped and got killed at the same moment. Imagine the poor thing's feelings, whilst laughing in its sleeve at our hacks at the wrong limb, on being suddenly disturbed by a pointed stick. If it had kept quiet it would even then have been safe, but it so boiled over with indignation that it couldn't hold itself and came out. A whack with a stick ended the fun. From Blanket Bay we kept a well beaten dray path to the Parker, a beautiful river with rustic bridge. Here I left my companions and went on alone. On rounding a hill I saw what looked like a church on the top of a hill. I made my way to this and was welcomed in most hospitably by Kelsall, the telegraph operator. He was most cordial, gave me a good tea and a shakedown on the sofa.

Next day, Monday, in the morning I was shown round. Visited the caves and limestone grottoes and went up the lighthouse. The man in charge showed us the revolving apparatus. The light is called a revolving light of the first order, transmitting a flash once every minute. There are twenty-one lamps and it takes seven lamps to make a flash,

Above: Blanket Bay   Below: near Lavers Hill

so it will be perceived that the whole affair turns round in three minutes. The lighthouse is very short and stumpy-looking, but this gives additional strength. The walls are five feet thick and the tower is round.

The only residents on the Cape which is the southernmost part of Australia are those who have to be there in an official capacity, such as the telegraph operator, the man in charge of the lighthouse and his assistants. On taking leave of Kelsall I, of course, asked him what the bill was. He seemed quite annoyed at my doing so and asked me what I should think of a man who expected to be paid for a night's board and lodging by the only stranger he had seen for six months. His last few words raised my respect for him.

On Monday the 5th of January, three in the afternoon I left Cape Otway for Glenample, distant 40 miles. I had appointed to sleep that night at a hut about 8 miles from Cape Otway with a man who could tell me the track to Glenample. Accordingly I made for this hut. Having followed the coast line over the hills for 3 or 4 miles I came to the river Eyre. From where I stood on top of the high sea bank I had a fine view of the river. At first sight it looked like an immense bay of bright sand with a silvery thread of water glistening under the lofty bank at the other side of the sand bay. The water was only two or three feet deep so I had no difficulty in getting across.....

Tuesday January 6th: That night I slept like a top. The next morning at 7.30 I started. The man, Jim Anderson, said I would see a track going up a hill and I was to follow that to Princetown. Over the hills to river Johanna, previous to which I had crossed a small creek, and once beyond the Johanna and up a sandhill or two I got on to the track. It was just a narrow footpath eighteen inches wide and I couldn't expect it to be very clearly defined, as it had only once been crossed within the preceeding twelve months. It first kept along the edge of the cliffs, but gradually edging off to my astonishment, it struck clean away into the forest, apparently on the top of a dividing range. After walking twelve miles or so in this direction without hardly seeing the sun, the foliage became so dense as to completely cover the path, all of a sudden, as it seemed to me, it turned gradually round and made for the coast through forest characterised by larger trees, but not such a dense undergrowth. This made the track harder to distinguish than before and often when it branched into two or three narrow paths I was in dread lest I should take a wrong turning and get off the proper road. I never once hesitated, but always went straight ahead and to this fact I owe my getting to the Gellibrand that night.

I feel now what a dangerous walk it was; in fact it almost makes me shudder to think how easily I could have left the path for may be death.....The cattle track still led me and it gradually became more well beaten, till I saw a cleared place to which it was going. To my great joy I discovered a nice cottage, empty; and from an old barrel half full with rusty water I had a glorious drink. This was about half past 5 p.m.. Ten hours is along time to go without water, walking all the time and I suffered greatly.

Set up now I went on my way. At another hut I met a young fellow and from him I learnt that the river which I now saw was the Gellibrand and that if I couldn't see anybody who would take me over in a boat he would be going across in an hour

Above: beach at Sherbrook River   Below: view from Cape Otway

1. *Cape Otway Lighthouse*
   Built: 1848 Height: 20 metres
   Tours: Tel. 052 379 240
2. *Aireys Inlet Lighthouse*
   Built: 1891 Height: 34 metres
3. *Cape Nelson Lighthouse*
   Built: 1884 Height: 32 metres
   Tours: tel. 055 232 671
4. *Point Lonsdale Lighthouse*
   Built: 1902 Height: 21 metres
5. *Queenscliff White Lighthouse*
   Built: 1863 Height: 22 metres
6. *Port Fairy Lighthouse*
   Built: 1859 Height: 12.5 metres
7. *Queenscliff Black Lighthouse*
   Built: 1863 Height: 24 metres
8. *Portland Lighthouse. Built: 1859*
   at Battery Point, moved 1890 to
   Whalers Point Height: 12 metres

and then I could navigate it on his horse. As I expected, nobody was about, so I waited for this verdant youth and in a couple of hours or so, about 8 o'clock, he turned up.....The horse refused to go a step further and stood there with its forelegs and chest in the water and its hind legs on dry land. I swore that if anybody got ducked it would be the driver and whilst urging him to propel his steed, the latter turned sharp round and came out onto dry land.

It was now quite dark and it was necessary to hurry if I wanted to get in to Mrs. Gibson's before they had shut up. I told the grinning idiot to cross when he could and I would go for a boat hunt. I followed the bank of the river up a good distance and fortunately came across a boat with two oars in it. I put myself across the river and then rode behind the chap on horseback up to Mrs Gibson's. I was dead beat and nearly killed with jolting. Only one light was visible. I gave a timid knock at the door. A lady's voice replied 'Who's there?' My nervous response gained me admittance and after a most hospitable reception, and a good tea went to a warm bed. The total distance I had walked today was 35 miles.

Next morning, Wednesday, I didn't get up till late, I was so tired, and after breakfast talked with a young lady, a Miss Jessie Curdie, 3rd daughter of Dr. Curdie of Tandarook, till dinner. She is 5 feet four, 8 stone 6, with a good figure, pleasing face, nice voice and most fascinating manners.

Mrs. Gibson is very kind. The house [Glenample Homestead] is a stone one and is situated on the sea side of a hill sloping upwards to the sea bank. The front view takes in the view of the country as far as the eye can reach towards Camperdown etc.

In the afternoon went down on the beach with Miss Curdie. Mr Gibson had cut in the perpendicular face of the cliff stone steps leading down to the beach and also has had excavated a famous tunnel cut through solid rock of a headland to make accessible another stretch of beach beyond. The cliffs all about here and for miles round are perfectly perpendicular, at places having immense gorges, also with perpendicular sides, running into the land and nearly always washed by the sea waves.

The most peculiar characteristic, however, is the number of immense rocks, or rather detached cliffs, standing right away from the land and surrounded with reefs, all about the coast. Many of these must be the size of a large church and of course have never been climbed.....

Wednesday January 14th: In afternoon went across to Gellibrand, a very pretty river. The view, with the river lying placid before me, the low sea bank on the one side and huge Point Ronald opposite casting a shadow on the water with the sun just sinking behind it, was delightful. Had a row, very windy and in evening, service in the dining room. This morning Mr. Tait and all went again to the beach and they all went away about dinner time. Walked across to the wreck. The gorge into which Tom Pearce and Miss Carmichael were washed is about 150 yards to the right, that is the west of where the Loch Ard struck. The Gorge running in first has a narrow opening which gradually widens till it is met by a headland running out from the land

Above: the Arch   Right & previous page: the Twelve Apostles

which divides it into two other gorges, the west one being ever so much longer and deeper than the eastern one. At the furthest end of both these gorges there is a cave in which can be found fresh water. The celebrated cave, however, is just round the first corner to the west arriving in from the sea. It runs straight out in the direction of the sea for a distance of seventy-five yards. The whole of the gorge is apparently very shallow and there is a fine broad beach. Each of the sub-gorges is covered with shrubs and stunted bushes that have taken root in the sand.

The beach is accessible only by means of steps cut down the headland into the west gorge and it was at the extremity of the headland, also on the west that Tom Pearce scaled. The tree that Miss Carmichael hid herself under is now a single stem of a beech tree and is at the foot of the steps. The caves are very pretty, of lime formation, water dripping through the ceiling having formed pretty little stalactites. They are very cold and are said to be the home of bats. The smaller gorges are covered with wreckage and a fine spar was on the beach. Strange to say, this was the only gorge for miles where a human being could be washed up in safety........

About a quarter of a mile to the West of the Loch Ard Gorge is the famous blowhole. This is an immense pit in the ground, sixty yards long ten – thirty broad and c. fifty feet deep; in shape similar to the gorges on the sea coast, except that it communicates with the sea by a huge subterranean tunnel over one hundred yards long. It seems to run still further inland underground, but it cannot be known with certainty; the waves dash into this blowhole and go roaming on into the other tunnel with a surging roar and splashing round that can be heard some way off. To fall in would be certain death........

Thursday January 15th: Thursday a lovely day. I say goodbye to Mrs Gibson with many thanks for the great hospitality she has shown me. I start away about 11 a.m. My road of course, as far as the Sherbroke is over the bald hills by the track which I have crossed often lately........

Port Campbell I came upon quite unexpectedly. I could see before I ascended the final hill, houses away up river, but I didn't know till coming down the hill I came upon a large house, evidently a store, that the bay I saw was in fact Port Campbell and the creek was Campbell's creek.

The scenery about was a great change from the everlasting bald prospect. The bay is broad and deep and runs in a good distance. The water in it is very deep and there is excellent anchorage. It is not, however, a safe port, being too much exposed to the south and S.W. winds and there is also some difficulty in getting into it, owing to a reef of rocks which runs out from the east extremity to a distance of a mile.......

On leaving the Port I kept along the edge of the cliffs for some time till the walk became so laborious that I cut away to the N.W. and fell in with the road again.The scene never varied. Away to my right were scattered clumps of trees usually near springs, to my left were bald hills covered with stunted bushes. This was for five miles. Then the country became more thickly timbered with wretched wattles, and the sheoak made its appearance. A gorge here, near a fence, was one of the finest I have ever seen. In shape it was a Port Campbell, in appearance it was like

Above: Loch Ard Gorge   Below: Mutton Bird Island and Loch Ard Gorge

Above and below: Sentinel Rock near Port Campbell

where the Loch Ard was wrecked. From the appearance of the coast I inferred I was getting near some large river, sandy hills having taken the place of the previous bald ones. I did not, however, expect to come upon such a large lake as I did. It stretched away out of sight up to my right and from where I stood it seemed to be about a mile across.....Running out from the shore into the sea is a low sandy spit, and at the furthest extremity of this is a rock named the Schomburgh rock which marks the spot where a vessel of the name of Schomburgh was wrecked. On the lake or inlet were an immense number of swans. In one mob quite close I counted 157. The west side of the bay that forms an entrance into the Curdie's inlet is remarkably rocky and studded with reefs.....

Walking along every now and then you catch a glimpse of the inhospitable coast. Always the water washed cliffs, with the huge detached rocks and sea dashing round them. I pass by the first house I come to and keep on over a sandy road till I come to a large house standing among a lot of ferns. I feel sure this is Irvine's and go across to see. On my telling my name he asked me in to dinner. Before doing so he took me across to show me the bay of islands. There is nothing very remarkable in this. Just an inlet divided with lofty detached cliffs. The centre one of all is called Lot's Wife.....Mr. Irvine says I am uneducated because I do not go in for Poetry, Sketching and Phrenology. He shows me original specimens of the two former and they excite my admiration. He tells me he looks at everything in the humorous light and versifies after the same style as Mark Twain in the Innocents Abroad. My head is examined. I have strong moral character, never swear, teetotaller, and keen sense of the ridiculous. Have no amativeness, combativeness, but strong religious feelings. I would make a good parson or a merchant as I have a good business head, am steady and of sedentary inclinations. There is no use my trying to be a doctor as I have neither courage, energy, endurance, determination nor self esteem.....

Below and above: London Bridge, before and after 1990

Saturday January 17th: Reaping was just going on. I had walked today about 18 miles, 6 miles to Irvine's, 10 to Mrs Palmer's and 2 to Wilson's. Saturday had a slight tendency to be wet and I had my misgivings when I started to walk the 12 miles to Warrnambool.....The west hills gradually became lower till they seem to run down into the sea. Quite close to me is Warrnambool on this sandy sort of ledge. From here the road is very pretty with the Hopkins in the foreground and the tree-surrounded houses on its banks. The road takes me to the Hopkins Bridge where I have dinner and which is 180 yards long. In an hour after, I walk into Warrnambool. My unusual garb excites astonishment in the minds of the people and a feeling that I am ridiculous in myself, so I lose no time in allaying both. I try to get a map; cannot. Also find there are no letters. Warrnambool is a very lively looking place with cabs and exceptionally fine hotels.

I am again on the mainroad, this time bound for a Mr. McLaws to an adopted daughter of whom I have a letter of introduction.....I cut across fields to a lofty hill [Tower Hill] with a telegraph line on the top.....Living here and owning the place is a kind old man, a retired publican, Mr. David McLaws. Having no children of his own and his wife being dead, he has adopted three sisters and one brother called Love. I was told the girls were rather colonial, so I did not expect much. They were the most ridiculously loud gawks I ever met. The quantity of 'H's dropped by the two younger was amply compensated for by the extraordinary rapidity of manufacture of them by the eldest sister. Their names are Lizzie, Maggie and Teeny, short for Christina. The second one is engaged to a draper's assistant. In return for Mr. McLaws keeping them, they are his servants, do the washing cooking etc.....

Sunday January 18th: I left soon after dinner and walked round the lake until I got into a road which took me on and on till I eventually got out on to the low sandy coast hills. I then went on to the beach and walked barefoot

as far as Belfast [Port Fairy]. The sea was out and the beach fine and hard. When near a land mark I came over the ridge and walked along the road into Belfast, crossing by a bridge the river Moyne. I saw two men and a goose and am stopping at a second rate inn. Between Warrnambool and Belfast the bay is called Port Fairy.....

The river Moyne before entering the sea forms into two branches enclosing an island. The eastern branch is navigable for small vessels up to the town. At the extremity of the island is a red lighthouse. Belfast is very dull.....The best hotel is the Star of the West. The one I am stopping in is about the worst. I had breakfast at 6.30 and started away about 7.00. My bill is 4 shillings. From Belfast to Portland is 43 miles. I follow the main road and telegraph poles for 12 miles till I get to Yambuk and was within a mile or two of the coast all the time. The line of hills on my left was sparsely wooded. Lying dead in the middle of the road I passed a snake about 3 1/2 feet long. I suspect it was a tiger snake. Yambuk is a small straggling bush township with a hotel or two, a couple of stores, a church, schoolhouse and post office.....

Tuesday January 20th: My walk yesterday was 31 miles. The day promised to be a regular scorcher. Somehow or other I didn't feel at all in good trim for walking and every few minutes I had to lay down and rest. The country was well timbered and pretty.....The last post town was Tyrendarra. I still walked on though the heat was intense and the hot winds scorching. I called in at a house to see if I could get some fruit and chummed in with the owner, an old digger, Frederick Saunders. He came to Portland 43 years ago, so he says, and shortly afterwards came to his present habitation. He has seen some stirring life on the diggings and has a vivid recollection of it. He had no fruit, but directed me to try across the road at another house. Here I bought 7 1/2 pounds of apricots and had a good feed. I had still 14 miles to go, so I started away again about 3. Bush fires were all about up in the ranges, travelling fast towards me. The smoke spoilt the view. The road I was on took me straight to where I could get a view of the sea and then turned away to the right parallel with the coast. For four miles now the country was perfectly flat and there was not a tree under which I could get shelter, nearer than ranges on my right.....

Below: Bay of Martyrs

    I wasn't long now getting on to the mainroad and as it was very late hurried on like the mischief. After walking 2 miles I got into Portland and stopped at the first hotel I met. I was too tired to eat anything, so asked for my room. Some distance had to be gone over uncarpeted stairs and balcony till I got to it. The flies were frightful, the room smelt horribly. I therefore opened the window as high as it would go and jumped into one of the beds. There were two others in the room. The fleas were in countless numbers. In the morning I wasn't called till breakfast was finished, so all I got was some cold fish recooked, old bread and rancid butter. My bill came to 2/6. Perhaps it will be as well to remember the name of the house of dirt. It was the 'Lamb' hotel owned by a S. McConachy, who told me he was a friend of my father's. I strolled about before leaving. Portland is a flourishing place and is connected by railway with Melbourne. The bay especially is very fine and there is a long new wharf situated between the old wharf and a tumbledown bathing house.

On the Point to the left is a wreck that has been there since long before the first white man settled in Portland. On the point to the right is the flagstaff and lighthouse. The best hotels are Mac's fronting the bay, Paramon's also fronting the bay and late residence of Mr. Henty and the London hotel.....

The country as you go on becomes more open and a great part of it is under cultivation. After passing several houses you come on to the top of a hill from where you can see Cape Bridgewater, a comparatively narrow neck of land running out in to the sea. A branch road takes you out on the E. side of this at the foot of a range of hills, quite bare and pigeonholed with rabbit burrows. You cannot see McKinley's house till you come to the end of this road, when you see it on the side of the cape, fronting you with the sea between. One or two other houses are behind it. I went up to the house and presented my letter from Mrs. Begg. McKinley said he had no room in the house at first but soon recollected that he could give me a shakedown. I was very hungry so had a glorious tea in the kitchen. I was strolling about afterwards and went down on to the rocks, to a hut where I saw some men. These are fishermen engaged in pursuit of Haddock or Trevalla. There are 18 in all; their boats are wretched little things and they are not born fishermen at all, being sons of farmers. Afterwards I was accosted by a military looking fellow, who asked me one or two questions. I told him who I was and what I was travelling for. He immediately became very friendly and without the slightest reserve told me that he was the State School teacher and had done trips similar to mine for many years in New Zealand. He introduced me to a squatter from the Wimmera stopping here, a Mr. Wettenhall, a short sturdy looking little fellow with a very pleasing face. The manner of introduction was characteristic "Mr. Wettenhall this is Mr. Morrison who to my mind is doing a very plucky thing. He has walked all the way from Queenscliff round the coast and intends to go on to Adelaide. What makes it all the more plucky is that he is

seventeen years of age and has never done anything like it before.".....

Mr. Chas L. Money, the schoolmaster, is an extraordinary man. In appearance he is 5 feet 11 inches high, broad shouldered and remarkably well made. He has fair hair, blue eyes an energetic nose and determined mouth. He is of a very impetuous disposition, very impatient of rebuke. He is 40 years of age, but being so fashionably dressed and wearing such a handsome moustache easily might be mistaken for 25.....

He has been several things in Victoria, was at the diggings, was a swagman and at another time was a traveller for a photographer. Nine years ago he received a situation at the Geelong Grammar School. He got drunk and was dismissed. He has been a teetotaller since, is now earning £100 a year as a State School teacher and is engaged to be married to a girl who subscribes herself in her letters 'Your loving little kitten.'

Not withstanding Mr. McKinley professed his inability to make me comfortable, I could not have been more so. In the morning before breakfast we men had a bathe in the sea. The breakers were glorious and it was very enjoyable. Cape Bridgewater is the western extremity of deep bay, the other cape opposite being Cape Nelson. McKinley's house is situated on the slope of this high headland, looking towards Cape Nelson. Below is a rocky beach, but at the head of the bay is a long strip of beautiful sand. The bay is the finest I have ever seen. It is protected by high hills, the majority of which are covered with the usual vegetation seen near the sea – but there is one strip about a mile long on the E. side of the bay of perfectly white sand mountains.

In the morning I went with Wettenhall and Thomson, taking McKinley as guide, to see some fine caves at the end of the cape. The scenery about is fine and rugged. The first cave is entered by an opening, to get to which you have to scramble up a place 6 feet high and as steep as the side of a house. It is about 20 or 30 yards long, of lime

Above: Bay of Islands   Below: Discovery Bay Coastal Park

stone formation, and therefore ornamented with the usual stalactites. The other cave is like a huge and lofty hall and does not run in very far.

In the afternoon I went much further round the coast to see some blowholes. Nothing I have seen anywhere round the coast can be even compared with the sublime scenery thereof. It was a calm day when I saw it, yet often when the waves struck the rocks they would send up a cloud of spray far above our heads and we were sitting 80 feet above the water on a ledge of rock. The cliffs here are of a dark blue colour, in formation and general appearance. On a rough day you cannot come near the top of the cliffs at all or you would be wet through instantly.

We saw two blowholes. Immediately after a wave thunders up against the rocks a huge puff of steam, smoke or water shoots out of these holes with a noise like a cannon. The rougher the weather, the louder the explosion. The waves are sublime they are magnificent. By Jerusalem I wish I could describe them. I know I could have looked at them for hours without getting tired. Mr. Money can't go near the edge of the cliffs, as he is seized with an irresistible desire to throw himself in and several times it has been all he could do to prevent himself. McKinley certainly feeds you well. His wife is an old tarter woman and everlasting talker and wears spectacles.

Friday January 23rd: I asked her how much there was to pay. 'Would a shilling a meal be too much, Sir?' Only 7 shillings. I left about 9.30 and was accompanied by Mr. Wettenhall, Mr. Thomson and McKinley. We were bound for some lakes near the coast on the western side of Cape Bridgewater. A walk of 6 miles over hills and sand brought us to them. The rabbits were about in swarms. Some curious caves on the side of a hill are worth seeing....

Saturday January 24th: Hedditch's house is 24 miles from Portland and three miles further on is a sly grog accommodation house owned by one Johnstones. I got a glass of brandy here which did me good. Through his paddock runs a stream of beautiful water. About 35 miles from Portland, a short distance off the road on the left, is a spring of water which tasted very much of the swamp. I took a billy full of it with me, but getting tired of carrying it, threw it away. Shortly afterwards I met a fellow traveller bound for Johnstone's. He was very thirsty, but I couldn't relieve him. Kangaroos are very plentiful. I also saw some large birds, black with apparently a hood on, and I believe they were black cockatoos. The Glenelg is 44 miles from Portland and is crossed by a punt. The man that works the punt has been down there 30 years on the 19th February. His name is Brown and for the convenience of visitors he has erected a large white stone house. I went to bed immediately on getting there and in the morning I had breakfast inside.

The Glenelg is a beautiful river, very broad and deep. In the distance about a mile away I could see the beach and people walking on it. The banks are high, especially on the western side. I was told there is some very fine scenery high up the river. I have now walked from Queenscliff to the Punt, a distance of 329 miles and I have resolved to go on to Adelaide.

Below: Glenelg River at Nelson   Right: the Blowholes, Cape Bridgewater

By the close of the 18th century exploration of Victoria's coast was underway. In the early 1800s the French and English were almost shadowing one another's vessels in the quest to chart the area and gain advantage for future claims. The most remarkable effort though, was by Matthew Flinders and George Bass. Unbelievably, these two dedicated navigators made initial explorations in a mere dinghy, 2.5 metres long, and aptly named the Tom Thumb. Although they did not venture far from Port Jackson, the experience was sufficient to prepare Bass for a voyage of nearly 1,000 kilometres to Western Port Bay, in an open whale-boat.

Successively larger vessels took them further afield with each journey and resulted in progressively more significant discoveries, in particular that of the strait between Victoria and Tasmania and named after Bass. Its discovery reduced sea-passage from England by a week. Ultimately it was the search for whales and seals that led to settlement along the south-west coast of Victoria, most notably at Portland. It was an industry that flourished until the 1840s, then waned as over-hunting exhausted supply.

During the middle part of the century a multitude of immigrants were coming to Australia. Initially demand for pastoral labour started the flow, but the rush for gold turned it into a flood. This wave of migration sent an endless stream of ships, bound for Melbourne and passing close by the coast. All too often, too close. Over 150 ships lie wrecked between Port Phillip Heads and the South Australian border. In time, a flourishing network of coastal traders was established, plying the waters with supplies for the settlements, and providing passage to Melbourne. For travellers the voyage from Warrnambool, at about two days, was immeasurably quicker than the overland route, though a little more hazardous at times.

Lorne and Apollo Bay started out as isolated settlements in the 1840s, both as a result of ships seeking shelter in their protected bays. Despite the coastline being surveyed in 1846 they remained reliant on the sea for supplies. Curiously, however, the telegraph line linking Tasmania with Melbourne in 1859 made the possibility of overland travel more feasible. The cable passed through Geelong and Winchelsea, as a telegraph wire above ground, then turned south to Moggs Creek. From there it followed the coast all the way to the telegraph station at Cape Otway, then crossed Bass Strait under the sea via King Island. However, for the most part, the track following the mainland coastal section was only traversable by foot or horse.

HISTORY OF THE GREAT OCEAN ROAD

The next development was a railway which opened in 1876 between Geelong and Winchelsea, where a coach service connected with Lorne. The first proposals for an ocean road between Geelong and Lorne came about in the 1880s, but were defeated because defence authorities thought it might make the area vulnerable to invasion. Besides, finance was unobtainable after the 1890s bank crash. The establishment of the Country Roads Board (CRB) in 1912, and its subsequent commitment to employ returned servicemen (from World War I) for road construction proved to be a great stimulus. The government recognized that little had been done to adequately service the numerous, and often economically significant, settlements along the south-west coast of Victoria. The final impetus, however, for realization of the project came from community support and resulted in the formation of the Great Ocean Road Trust in 1918. Influentially, it included members of both state and local government and the CRB. Funds were raised and planning commenced as a private enterprise. Construction started on the first section between Lorne and Cape Paton in 1919, carried out by the CRB for the Trust.

Progress was slow and arduous in the extreme, especially for the thousands of returned soldiers employed, many of them debilitated by war. For the most part, tools of construction were picks, shovels and crow bars. Some suggested prison labour might be more appropriate for the task. The section from Eastern View to Lorne was opened in 1922, with a toll applied to vehicles using it, and in 1932 the entire road between Anglesea and Apollo Bay was completed. The Memorial Arch at Eastern View was originally built in 1939 with a plaque bearing the inscription: "the road was built to commemorate the services of those who served in the Great War". Owing to fire, tempest and a misguided truck, the arch has been rebuilt several times since, most recently in 1991.

The name "Great Ocean Road" was originally applied to the stretch between Anglesea and Apollo Bay, and its construction was regarded as a significant achievement in view of the engineering feat it represented at the time. The consequences were enormous for the townships dotted along its route, especially in the area of tourism, for the road was in fact the creation of a coastal scenic drive that rivalled any in the world. *Picture: the Falls of Halladale at Massacre Bay near Peterborough, 1908*

In 1878 Captain Gibb sailed for Melbourne in a three-masted, iron-hulled clipper of 1,693 tons. Among the more unusual items of cargo on the Loch Ard was a valuable porcelain peacock, 1.5 metres high, bound for exhibitions in Sydney and Melbourne. The clipper provided excellent accommodation for 17 passengers, eight of whom were from one family, the Carmichaels.

At 4 a.m. on June 1st, while the crew were unable to take accurate bearings because of haze, the Loch Ard was swept onto a reef extending from Mutton Bird Island. Masts and rigging smashed onto the deck,

along with huge limestone rocks from the cliff-face, trapping passengers and crew below. Many had already been thrown into the raging sea. Eighteen year old Tom Pierce, an apprentice seaman, who could swim, clung to an upturned life-boat. He was swept into the narrow entrance of a deep gorge, surrounded by 50 metre high cliffs. Eva Carmichael, also aged 18 years, could not swim, however she clung to a chicken coop for nearly four hours and then to a spar. She was also miraculously washed into the same gorge. Tom, while lying on the beach in a state of exhaustion heard Eva's cries from the sea, and despite his weak condition he swam out to rescue her. After struggling for over an hour he managed to bring the by now semi-conscious Eva to shore. He lay her in a cave, covered her in foliage in the hope of warming her, and gave her brandy found amongst the wreckage on the beach.

Then with enormous difficulty, he scaled the cliff. After wandering aimlessly for some hours, dazed by a wound on the head, he met two drovers from nearby Glenample station and told them of the wrecked Loch Ard. The manager of Glenample, Hugh Gibson, organized a rescue party and Eva was brought to the homestead where with warmth and rest she recovered from her shocking ordeal. Sadly for the romantically minded public, she did not marry Tom Pearce, but returned to Ireland, where she married someone else six years later.

Tom, who was awarded with a gold medal for bravery by the Royal Humane Society returned to England ultimately to become a master of steamships. He miraculously survived several more shipwrecks until his death at 47 years of age. The extraordinary story of the Loch Ard has fascinated people for well over a century. Fifty-two lives were lost, but amazingly the porcelain peacock was washed ashore unharmed and is now displayed in the Warrnambool Maritime Museum.

In the early 1850s a ship was built in Aberdeen to challenge the record breaking clippers of North America. The Schomberg was expected to be the fastest ship in the world, weighing 2,600 tons and carrying over three acres of sail. On October 6th, 1855, she left Liverpool under the command of Captain

James "Bully" Forbes, one of the most highly regarded seaman in the world and renowned for fast passage under sail. Over 300 passengers were accommodated in the lavishly decorated clipper. They enjoyed a library of 400 books, velvet pile carpets, mahogany furniture and sixty luxurious staterooms. Built at a cost of £43,000 it was the pride of the fleet and actually capable of carrying 1,000 passengers. The cargo for the voyage included 2,000 tons of rail for the Geelong to Melbourne railway.

In the early hours of boxing day, after a journey marred by becalming, and thus taking far longer than the 60 days boasted of by the captain on departing Liverpool, the Schomberg inexplicably ran aground in calm sea, 250 metres from the shore of Peterborough. None of the several enquiries (including criminal charges laid against Captain Forbes) discovered just why the ship coasted along a shore known to be extremely dangerous and imperfectly chartered. A passing coastal steamer rescued all on board as well as 17,000 letters to waiting Victorians.

Although not greatly harmed when run aground, three days later gales caused the ship to gradually break up and she was ultimately destroyed. (The bow section had drifted to New Zealand by 1870.) Many rumours surrounded the behaviour and judgement of the captain at the time of the disaster. Some said he was on deck, but this was hard to believe as he could so easily have averted the grounding. Others said he was below deck entertaining the doctor and various attractive ladies. Whatever the truth, his reputation was ruined and the magnificent Schomberg was lost on her maiden voyage. *Picture: etching of the Loch Ard tragedy*

NATIONAL PARKS & STATE PARKS

About one third of the coastline between Port Phillip Heads and the South Australian border is national, state or coastal parkland. This is a crucial factor in preserving the unique nature of the glorious landscape through which the Great Ocean Road sweeps. At each of the parks, information sheets describing points of interest and walking tracks are obtainable from the park office. The walks suggested on the sheets are always described in detail, with maps. Where there is no office there is usually a display board and a box nearby containing the information sheets. Camping is permitted in the majority of parks. The facilities are detailed in the section in this book on National and State Park Camping Grounds. Domestic animals and firearms are prohibited in all the parks; however, in the case of dogs there are some exceptions. The overriding one is that it is acceptable for dogs to be left in the car whilst their owners are visiting the sights, but only in the course of travelling through a park via a main through-road, such as the Great Ocean Road. Fires are allowed only in fireplaces where provided (exceptions are detailed in the case of Aire River, Johanna and Princetown). All native plants and animals are protected by law and it is an offence to damage or remove any specimens, including rocks and soil.

ANGAHOOK LORNE STATE PARK

The park begins at Aireys Inlet and follows the spine of the Otway Ranges until Kennett River. Its steep, timbered slopes to the water's edge are a striking feature all the way along the park, and it is these in particular that originally gave the Great Ocean Road its reputation as one of the finest scenic routes in the world. The park's numerous coves and sandy beaches are often characterized by rock platforms between sand and sea. Properly described in the main part as a cool temperate rainforest, the park boasts a wealth of waterfalls and a network of well made and clearly signposted walking tracks. The eastern and drier part, around Aireys Inlet, includes heathland with abundant wildflowers in spring and early summer. This area is especially renowned for its native orchids. Camping is permitted at five locations and there are numerous picnic grounds in forest settings. In 1983 the fires of Ash Wednesday desolated a large part of the park east of Lorne through to Anglesea. Fortunately no plant species were lost and the wildlife has made a remarkable recovery, though it will be many years yet before the ecological balance is re-established.

OTWAY NATIONAL PARK

Located to the west of Apollo Bay, the park covers a large tract of temperate rainforest between Hordern Vale and Blanket Bay. Near Cape Otway the park becomes confined to the coast, becoming a continuous narrow strip all the way to Princetown, though often inaccessible. The Otways have the highest rainfall in the state, in places over 2000 millimetres annually. The rainforest is best known for its towering mountain ash, one of the world's tallest trees, growing up to 100 metres high. One of the best places to observe the forest is at Maits Rest, by way of a 45 minute walk. It includes sections of raised boardwalk with informative signs, where you can wander through a veritable sea of tree ferns, with moss clinging to everything in this seemingly saturated environment. Some ancient myrtle beeches have developed extraordinary forms (a few in the park are estimated to be 2000 years old), whilst every now and again a mountain ash of monumental scale soars out of sight. Beyond Cape Otway, the terrain of the park starts to vary significantly as its area stretches out over a considerable distance. The coastline along this section is most easily accessible at Aire River, Glenaire, Johanna Beach, Moonlight Head and Princetown. There are six camping grounds and two designated picnic spots in the park, one at Shelly Beach (known as the Elliot River Picnic Ground), the other at Blanket Bay.

MELBA GULLY STATE PARK

This park, (a mere 48 hectares), is located just west of Lavers Hill. The original property was named after Dame Nellie Melba and donated to the state in 1975. Early in the century there were two sawmills operating in the gully and during the 1930s and 40s tea-rooms on the property provided a popular tourist stop-over and picnic spot. The current picnic ground is on the site of the tea-rooms and is provided with wood BBQs and toilets. Leading off from this open area is a looped nature walk taking about 35 minutes to complete. The walk passes through a gully of dense forest comprising myrtle beech, blackwood and tree ferns, with an understorey of low ferns and mosses. It has a lot in common with the Maits Rest Track, but is much dimmer and even more saturated. At night it becomes quite atmospheric while viewing the glow worms for which the park is most famous. They are actually a species of small fly at the larval stage of growth and make sticky threads that trap insects attracted by their glow. Wooden bridges along the track cross the Johanna River, cascading in parts, and at the top of a set of steps is the Big Tree, a messmate some 300 years old and 27 metres in girth. Camping is not permitted in the park.

Loch Ard Gorge

PORT CAMPBELL NATIONAL PARK

Stretching from Princetown to Peterborough, Port Campbell National Park is a mostly narrow strip of coastal heathland lying between the Great Ocean Road and the sea. The park offices at Port Campbell include an information centre, natural history displays and an audio-visual presentation describing the spectacular coastline. Though best known for the Twelve Apostles island rock formation, the park boasts numerous other spectacles of nature etched into the limestone cliffs, in places providing sheer drops of 70 metres. Loch Ard Gorge is famous for the wreck in 1878 of the *Loch Ard*, a three-masted clipper wrecked off Mutton Bird Island with the loss of 52 lives. The island is named for its rookery of mutton birds, a migratory bird that can be seen returning to the island each night at dusk, between September and May. Nearby are the Blowhole, Loch Ard Cemetery and Thunder Cave, all linked by numerous walking tracks that connect to Loch Ard Gorge. Both the Twelve Apostles and London Bridge have fairy penguin colonies, each isolated and protected by the cliffs. At dusk they return in their hundreds from a day of feeding and can be seen from the viewing platforms. At Port Campbell a discovery walk along the cliff's edge, beside the bay, takes in spectacular views all the way to Two Mile Bay, where shell middens are evidence of Aboriginal occupation and their long association with the coastline. Camping in the park is only allowed at the Port Campbell Caravan Park.

TOWER HILL STATE GAME RESERVE

The idyllic form of Tower Hill and its volcanic crater, now a lake, was preserved in its original beauty in an oil painting by Eugene von Guerard in 1855. Sadly, by 1861 much of the land had been cleared of timber, and subsequently as natural vegetation disappeared so did the birds and mammals. Moves to protect the area resulted in Tower Hill being declared Victoria's first national park in 1892, becoming a state game reserve in 1961. Using von Guerard's painting as a blueprint, a unique experiment in revegetation and wildlife recolonization began in 1961 to recreate an environment destroyed by man. Over 250,000 trees and shrubs have been planted, enticing back the birds and providing a new home for the mammals being reintroduced. There are now emus, koalas, kangaroos and echidnas roaming around, the emus definitely being the most friendly. A series of short walks take visitors around the reserve and there is a picnic ground with electric BBQs. The Natural History Centre includes displays of the local geology and revegetation program. It was designed by Robin Boyd and opened in 1971.

Melba Gully

MOUNT ECCLES NATIONAL PARK

This national park is like a huge oasis in the midst of vast tracts of farmland. The focus of interest is Lake Surprise, comprising three adjoining volcanic craters fed by underground springs. Clinging to the craggy cliffs surrounding the lake is a woodland of manna gums and blackwoods. The craters beneath the lake were formed as a result of volcanic activity some 20,000 years ago. The most recent eruption was less than 7,000 years ago, suggesting to volcanologists that it may not be completely extinct. Although Mount Eccles is 180 metres above sea level it appears more a hill than a mountain and was formed by lava exploding from the crater, solidifying into scoria and being blown eastwards. In fact it is barely a hill, considering past scoria quarrying has virtually sliced it in half. The park has a series of beautiful bush walks, parts of which are accessible to wheelchairs. The Crater Rim Nature Walk can be demanding in parts, but rewards walkers with the best views. There is also a large lava cave, so take a torch. Camping sites and picnic facilities (some undercover) are provided, along with toilets and even hot showers.

NATIONAL PARKS & STATE PARKS

CAPE NELSON STATE PARK
Cape Nelson State Park is a relatively small park, 11 kilometres south-west of Portland, at the tip of a head-land covered in coastal scrub and heathland. Its geographic prominence was cause for the location of its splendid lighthouse and surrounding compound, built in 1884. It is open to the public, with tours up the lighthouse tower at certain times. The area is accessible via Cape Nelson Road or the more interesting Scenic Road, off which is a picnic area with views of the lighthouse in the distance. The Great South West Walk follows the Cape's coastline along its craggy limestone cliffs. There is also a three kilometre Sea Cliff Nature Walk including points of interest described in park notes. Part of the reason the park exists is to protect the small soap mallee tree, otherwise only found in South Australia. Camping is not permitted.

MOUNT RICHMOND NATIONAL PARK
The entrance road leads you straight to the summit of Mount Richmond where there are picnic areas, toilets, an information board and best of all, a lookout tower that takes you up into the tree tops. Sensational 360 degree views of the countryside include the dunes of Discovery Bay, Portland and the smelter, and even the Grampians on a clear day. There are numerous walks of varying distance through the bush, and in particular the Ocean View Walk provides excellent vistas from a platform. Mount Richmond is an extinct volcano, though barely evident as such today, for most of it was covered with a layer of sand blown in from Discovery Bay long ago. About 450 species of plants have been recorded in the park, including 50 orchids. It has some of Victoria's best wildflowers, wonderfully colourful in spring, though there are plants flowering almost any time during the year. The park supports a wide range of wildlife including eastern grey kangaroos, koalas and emus. It is also an important habitat for the uncommon southern potoroo, a small member of the kangaroo family. Camping is not permitted.

DISCOVERY BAY COASTAL PARK
Just before Tarragal on Bridgewater Lakes Road, it is worth pulling over to take in the extraordinary vista of the sand dunes of Discovery Bay Coastal Park. They are an amazing expanse, several kilometres wide in places. The park is a narrow coastal strip of ocean beach and dunes, stretching from the South Australian border eastwards along the full length of Discovery Bay. The dunes have expanded somewhat since grazing and rabbits have removed vegetation, but natural erosion has also played a part and they are now a mass of mobile sand, forever shifting. Behind them are a series of small lakes, reedy swamps and heathland. The Great South West Walk follows the beach, with camping sites at Swan Lake, Lake Moniebeong and White Sands. Swimming is not recommended in the ocean, as it is a rough surf beach, whereas the lakes are suitable. Horse riding is allowed between Lake Moniebeong and Cape Bridgewater, and dune buggies are permitted in certain areas, but you must be a member of the Portland Dune Buggy Club. One of the best spots for observing birdlife is the estuary at Nelson where spoonbills, pelicans and swans can be seen. Along the ocean beaches gulls, dotterels and terns feed close to the waterline.

LOWER GLENELG NATIONAL PARK
Flowing through the greater part of the park is the Glenelg River, "the finest body of fresh water....in Australia", as the Surveyor General of New South Wales, Major Thomas Mitchell, wrote in 1836, on his historic expedition down the river. For 15 kilometres along its lower reaches, the river has carved out an impressive gorge through limestone, with cliffs 50 metres high. Typical of areas with a limestone geology, there are many caves in the vicinity, but only the Princess Margaret Rose Caves are open to the public. They are over 20 metres underground, 150 metres long and have an amazing array of stalactites and stalagmites. Surrounding the caves and display centre is a glorious parkland with walks along the Glenelg River, picnic and camping grounds, and even cabins. Upstream are a further 17 campsites, eight of which are accessible by car, the remainder only by canoe or walking. The Great South West Walk follows the river and is perfect for canoeing, which is an ideal way of observing the park's rich birdlife, especially the waterbirds. (Conservation & Natural Resources provide information sheets describing facilities and advice for canoeists.) Most of the national park is covered in eucalypt bushland, but the eastern end, being less fertile, has more heathland and a dazzling display of wildflowers.

Queenscliff

ATHELSTANE HOUSE
4 Hobson Street, Queenscliff, 3225
Tel. 052 581 591
Guest House / Bed & Breakfast (14 rooms)
Tariff: $50–$90 per night, per double incl. breakfast

MAYTONE BY THE SEA
Cnr Stevens Street & The Esplanade, Queenscliff, 3225
Tel. 052 584 059
Fax 052 584 071
Guest House / Bed & Breakfast (9 rooms)
Tariff: $90–$125 per night, per double incl. breakfast

OZONE HOTEL
42 Gellibrand Street, Queenscliff, 3225
Tel. 052 581 011
Fax 052 583 712
Hotel (22 rooms)
Tariff: $95–$120 per night, per double

THE QUEENSCLIFF HOTEL
16 Gellibrand Street, Queenscliff, 3225
Tel. 052 581 066
Fax 052 581 899
Hotel (24 rooms)
Tariff: $180–$232 per night, per double incl. breakfast & dinner

THE QUEENSCLIFF INN
59 Hesse Street, Queenscliff, 3225
Tel. 052 583 737
Fax 052 582 819
Guest House / Bed & Breakfast (14 rooms)
Tariff: $65–$80 per night, per double incl. breakfast

THE ROYAL HOTEL
34–38 King Street, Queenscliff, 3225
Tel. 052 581 669
Fax 052 581 828
Hotel (8 rooms)
Tariff: $60 per night, per double incl. breakfast

ACCOMMODATION

Queenscliff cont.

SEAVIEW GUEST HOUSE
86 Hesse Street, Queenscliff, 3225
Tel. 052 581 763
Bed & Breakfast (11 rooms)
Tariff: $60–$95 per night, per double incl. breakfast

SUMA PARK COTTAGES
Bellarine Highway, Marcus Hill, 3222
Tel. 052 583 507
10 cottages (each sleep 8)
Tariff: $100–$230 per night, 2 to 8 people respectively

VUE GRAND PRIVATE HOTEL
46 Hesse Street, Queenscliff, 3225
Tel. 052 581 544
Fax 052 583 471
Private Hotel (34 rooms)
Tariff: $180 per night, per double incl. breakfast

WANDA INN B&B
34 Mercer Street, Queenscliff, 3225
Tel. 052 581 537
Bed & Breakfast (1 room sleeps 4)
Tariff: $70 per night, per double incl. breakfast

Barwon Heads

THE BARWON HEADS GOLF CLUB
Golf Links Road, Barwon Heads, 3227
Tel. 052 542 302
Fax 052 543 270
Hotel style (17 rooms)
Tariff: $210 per night, per double incl. all meals. Accommodation
is available to members of the club and their guests, or properly
introduced visitors being members of registered golf clubs.

Torquay

CEDAR COTTAGE
545 Great Ocean Road, Bellbrae, 3221
Tel. 052 613 844
Cottage (sleeps 6)
Tariff: $50–$65 per night

ACCOMMODATION

Torquay cont.

DELATITE COUNTRY COTTAGES
815 Pettavel Road, Freshwater Creek, 3216
Tel. 052 645 296
3 cottages (each sleep 5)
Tariff: $90–$120 per night

GLENFIDDICH CABINS
125 Eaglepoint Road, Torquay, 3228
Tel. 052 661 442
3 cottages (each sleep 6)
Tariff: $60–$65 per night

Aireys Inlet

LIGHTKEEPER'S COTTAGES
Federal Street, Aireys Inlet, 3221
Tel. 052 896 306
Fax 052 896 306
2 cottages (sleep 4 & 6)
Tariff: $125–$140 per night

Birregurra

ELLIMINOOK B&B
Elliminook, Warncoort Road, Birregurra, 3242
Tel. 052 362 080
Fax 052 313 424
Bed & Breakfast (2 rooms sleep 4)
Tariff: $95 per night, per double incl. breakfast

Lorne

ALLENVALE COTTAGES
Allenvale Road, Lorne, 3232
Tel. 052 892 650
5 cottages (sleep 4 to 6)
Tariff: $75–$125 per night

ERSKINE FALLS COTTAGES
Erskine Falls Road, Lorne, 3232
Tel. 052 892 666
Fax 052 892 247
12 cottages (sleep 3 to 8)
Tariff: $60–$150 per night

ACCOMMODATION

Lorne cont.

GREAT OCEAN ROAD COTTAGES
Erskine Avenue, Lorne, 3232
Tel. 052 891 070
6 cottages (each sleep 5)
Tariff: $70–$150 per night

PENNYROYAL FARM COTTAGES
Pennyroyal Valley Road, Deans Marsh, 3235
Tel. 052 363 391
2 Cottages (sleep 4 & 7)
Tariff: $75 per night

PENNYROYAL VALLEY COTTAGES
Pennyroyal Valley Road, Deans Marsh, 3235
Tel. 052 363 201
3 Cottages (sleep 6, 8 & 16)
Tariff: $80–$100 per night, for the 2 smaller cottages

SHALOM COTTAGES
Division Road, Murroon, 3242
Tel. 052 363 328
3 Cottages (each sleep 4)
Tariff: $70–$95 per night

TURRAMURRA PARK
645 Pennyroyal Valley Road, Deans Marsh, 3235
Tel. 052 363 346
Group accommodation (8 rooms sleep 44)
Tariff: $300 minimum per night

Skenes Creek

CHRIS'S RESTAURANT & VILLAS AT BEACON POINT
Skenes Creek Road, Skenes Creek, 3233
Tel. 052 376 411
Fax 052 376 930
6 Apartments (each sleep 4 or more)
Tariff: $150–$200 per night

ACCOMMODATION

Skenes Creek

TANYBRYN TEA HOUSE & GALLERY B&B
Cnr Skenes Creek & Wild Dog Roads, Tanybryn, 3249
Tel. 052 376 271 (or fax)
Bed & Breakfast (2 rooms sleep 4)
Tariff: $80 per night, per double incl. breakfast

WONGARRA HEIGHTS B&B
Sunnyside Road, Wongarra, 3221
Tel. 052 370 257
Bed & Breakfast (5 rooms sleep 12)
Tariff: $80 per night, per double incl. breakfast

Apollo Bay

AILSA FABB B&B
Barham Valley Road, Apollo Bay, 3233
Tel. 052 376 013
Bed & Breakfast (2 rooms sleep 5)
Tariff: $50 per night, per double incl. breakfast

ARCADY HOMESTEAD B&B
Barham Valley Road, Apollo Bay, 3233
Tel. 052 376 493
Farmhouse / Bed & Breakfast (4 rooms sleep 9)
Tariff: $80 per night, per double incl. breakfast

Cape Otway

CAPE OTWAY LIGHTHOUSE ACCOMMODATION
Otway Lighthouse Road, Cape Otway
Tel. 052 379 240
Cottage (smaller part sleeps 2, larger part sleeps 8)
Tariff: $40–$150 per night

Glenaire

FORD RIVER FARMHOUSE
Great Ocean Road, Glenaire, 3238
Tel. 052 379 226
Tel. 03 723 1585 (or fax)
Farmhouse cottage (sleeps 8)
Tariff: $75 per night

Glenaire cont.

GLEN AIRE LOG CABINS
Great Ocean Road, Glenaire, 3238
Tel. 052 379 231
Fax 052 379 269
4 cottages (each sleep 6)
Tariff: $65–$100 per night

Johanna

BUSH HAVEN HOLIDAY CABIN
Red Johanna Road, Johanna, 3238
Tel. 052 374 245
Cottage (sleeps 5)
Tariff $60–$90 per night

JOHANNA SEASIDE HOLIDAY FARM
Red Johanna Road, Johanna, 3238
Tel. 052 374 242
2 cottages (sleep 6 & 8)
Tariff: $80–$135 per night

WANGERRIP HOLIDAY LODGES
Blue Johanna Road, Johanna, 3238
Tel. 052 374 226
3 cottages (each sleep 6)
Tariff: $90–$155 per night

Princetown

CLIFTON LODGE
Great Ocean Road, Princetown, 3269
Tel. 055 988 128
2 cottages (sleep 6 & 8)
Tariff: $45–$80 per night

PRINCETOWN COTTAGES
Great Ocean Road, Princetown, 3269
Tel. 055 988 103
2 cottages (each sleep 4)
Tariff: $45–$55 per night

ACCOMMODATION

Warrnambool

INJEMIRA COUNTRY HOUSE B&B
Injemira Road, Grassmere, 3282
Tel. 055 654 434
Bed & Breakfast (2 rooms sleep 4)
Tariff: $95 per night, per double incl. breakfast

RIVER VIEW FARM B&B
11 Duirs Street, Warrnambool, 3280
Tel. 055 611 216
Bed & Breakfast (1 room sleeps 2)
Tariff: $70 per night, per double incl. breakfast

WOLLASTON B&B
84 Wollaston Road, Warrnambool, 3280
Tel. 055 622 430
Bed & Breakfast (2 rooms sleep 4)
Tariff: $75–$90 per night, per double incl. breakfast

WOODFIELD COTTAGE B&B
Bushfield–Tower Hill Road, Bushfield, 3282
Tel. 055 621 927
Bed & Breakfast (2 rooms sleep 4)
Tariff: $75 per night, per double incl. breakfast

Port Fairy

CLONMARA B&B
106 Princes Highway, Port Fairy, 3284
Tel. 055 682 595
Bed & Breakfast (1 room sleeps 2)
Tariff: $85 per night, per double incl. breakfast

CONA B&B
Cnr Princes Highway & Villiers Street, Port Fairy, 3284
Tel. 055 681 000
Fax 055 681 616
Bed & Breakfast (2 rooms sleep 4)
Tariff: $70 per night, per double incl. breakfast

ACCOMMODATION

Port Fairy cont.

DUBLIN HOUSE RIVERSIDE COTTAGE
17 Gipps Street, Port Fairy, 3284
Tel. 055 681 822
Cottage (sleeps 4)
Tariff: $95–$140 per night

GOBLE'S MILLHOUSE B&B
75 Gipps Street, Port Fairy, 3284
Tel. 055 681 118
Bed & Breakfast (6 rooms sleep 12)
Tariff: $85–$120 per night, per double incl. breakfast

HANLEY HOUSE B&B
14 Sackville Street, Port Fairy, 3284
Tel. 055 682 709
Bcd & Breakfast (3 rooms sleep 8)
Tariff: $65 per night, per double incl. breakfast

KILKARLEN AT KILLARNEY B&B
Survey Lane, Killarney, 3282
Tel. 055 687 258
Bed & Breakfast / Self Cont. Accom. (2 rooms sleep 4)
Tariff: $85 per night, per double incl. breakfast

LAVENDER COTTAGE
13 Sackville Street, Port Fairy, 3284
Tel. 052 222 566
Fax 052 218 778
Cottage (sleeps 5)
Tariff: $60–$100 per night

LOUGH COTTAGE B&B
216 Griffiths Street, Port Fairy, 3284
Tel. 055 681 583
Bed & Breakfast (2 rooms sleep 4)
Tariff: $60 per night, per double incl. breakfast

Port Fairy cont.

MERRIJIG INN B&B
1 Campbell Street, Port Fairy, 3284
Tel. 055 682 324
Fax 055 682 436
Bed & Breakfast (5 rooms sleep 10)
Tariff: $85–$100 per night, per double incl. breakfast

RAILWAY COTTAGE
56 Gipps Street, Port Fairy, 3284
Tel. 055 681 838 (or fax)
Cottage (sleeps 6)
Tariff: $95–$120 per night

RIVERSIDE COTTAGES
41 Gipps Street, Port Fairy, 3284
Tel. 055 292 253 (or fax)
2 cottages (each sleep 4)
Tariff: $60–$100 per night

Yambuk

SEAWINDS B&B
Youls Road, Yambuk, 3285
Tel. 055 684 206
Bed & Breakfast (2 rooms sleep 4)
Tariff: $50 per night, per double incl. breakfast

Tyrendarra

TARABAH FARM HOUSE
School Road, Tyrendarra, 3285
Tel. 055 681 790
Farm House (3 rooms sleep 6)
Tariff: $60–$115 per night

Portland

BURSWOOD HOMESTEAD B&B
15 Cape Nelson Road, Portland, 3305
Tel. 055 234 686
Fax 055 235 293
Bed & Breakfast (5 rooms sleep 12)
Tariff: $85–$120 per night, per double
incl. breakfast, afternoon tea & light supper

ACCOMMODATION

Portland cont.

PORTLAND INN B&B
4 Percy Street, Portland, 3305
Tel. 055 232 985
Bed & Breakfast (3 rooms sleep 6)
Tariff: $85 per night, per double incl. breakfast

VICTORIA HOUSE
5–7 Tyers Street, Portland, 3305
Tel. 055 217 577
Fax 055 236 300
Private Hotel (9 rooms)
Tariff: $80–$90 per night, per double

Bridgewater Bay

BRIDGEWATER SEA VIEW LODGE
Bridgewater Road, Cape Bridgewater
Tel. 055 267 217
Bed & Breakfast (sleeps 5)
Tariff: $60 per night, per double incl. breakfast

SHELLY BEACH RETREAT
Bridgewater Road, Bridgewater Bay
Tel. 055 231 577
Cottage (sleeps 8)
Tariff: $70–$88 per night

SAINT PETERS CHURCH
Bridgewater Lakes Road, Bridgewater Bay
Tel. 055 267 271
Renovated National Trust Church (sleeps 6–8)
Tariff: $65–$85 per night

Nelson

CONTENTO COTTAGE
Cnr. Kellett & Sturt Streets, Nelson
Tel. 087 384 161
Guest House / Bed & Breakfast (7 rooms sleep 20)
Tariff: $40–$60 per night, per double incl. breakfast

ART GALLERIES

Geelong
Geelong Art Gallery
Little Malop Street, Geelong
Tel. 052 293 645

Queenscliff
Hobson's Choice Gallery
2 Hobson Street, Queenscliff
Tel. 052 582 161

Seaview Gallery
86 Hesse Street, Queenscliff
Tel. 052 583 645

Ocean Grove
The Cobblers Cottage Gallery
Dare Street,
Ocean Grove
Tel. 052 551 161

Torquay
Atelier Design Craft Centre
170 Bones Road, Bells Beach
Tel. 052 614 836

The Gallery
39 Geelong Road,
Torquay
Tel. 052 616 457

Anglesea
Melaleuca Gallery
121 Ocean Road, Anglesea
Tel. 052 631 230

Aireys Inlet
Lightkeepers Stables Tearoom
& Gallery
7 Federal Street, Aireys Inlet
Tel. 052 897 148

Fairhaven
Hidden Treasures
5 Cowan Avenue, Fairhaven
Tel. 052 896 886

Lorne
Qdos Fine Contemporary Art
60 Mountjoy Parade, Lorne
Tel. 052 891 989

Skenes Creek
Tanybryn Teahouse & Gallery
Skenes Creek Road,
Tanybryn
Tel. 052 376 271

Apollo Bay
Gumboot Gallery
Mechanics Hall,
Great Ocean Road, Apollo Bay
Open Friday to Monday &
daily during school holidays

Port Campbell
Port Campbell Trading
Company
Lord Street, Port Campbell
Tel. 055 986 444

Warrnambool
Customs House Gallery
Gilles Street, Warrnambool
Tel. 055 648 963

Robert Ulmann Studio
Hopkins Point Rd, Allansford
Tel. 055 651 444

Warrnambool Art Gallery
165 Timor Street, Warrnambool
Tel. 055 647 832

Port Fairy
Port Fairy Flower Gallery
23 Bank Street, Port Fairy
Tel. 055 682 222

Hot Glass Studio
62 Regent Street, Port Fairy
Tel. 055 682 794

Portland
Art Works
3 Henty Street, Portland
Tel. 055 233 037

Old State Bank Gallery
30 Percy Street, Portland
Tel. 055 233 337

Theatre Art Gallery
40 Julia Street, Portland
Tel. 055 231 117

BOAT CHARTERS & RIVER CRUISES

Queenscliff
Queenscliff Charters
2 Hesse Street, Queenscliff
Tel. 018 326 207

S.V.Wright
67 Learmonth Street,
Queenscliff
Tel. 052 581 762

Barwon Heads
Adamas
5 Bostock Avenue
Barwon Heads
Tel. 052 542 904

Apollo Bay
M.V.Revolution Charters
Fishermans Wharf, Apollo Bay
Tel. 03 793 3405

Port Campbell
Port Campbell Boat Charters
Lord Street, Port Campbell
Tel. 055 986 463 (bookings)
Tel. 055 985 401 (after hours)

Port Fairy
Sherilinda Cruises
14 Albert Street, Port Fairy
Tel. 055 681 619

Portland
Ra Charters
RMB 3242, Portland
Tel. 055 292 342
Tel. 018 514 304

Nelson
Glenelg River Cruises
Beach Road, Nelson
Tel. 087 384 192

"Nelson Endeavour" River
Cruises
c/- Nelson Post Office
Tel. 087 384 191

BUSHWALKS & WATERFALLS

For further details and maps of the walks listed below, contact the local Conservation and Natural Resources (C&NR) office, or the local information centre. If walking in winter it is best to check river and creek levels with the local C&NR office before setting out.

Ocean Grove
Ocean Grove Nature Reserve: Located to the north of the township and accessible from Grubb Road. There is a track that loops around the reserve, an easy 1 hour walk.

Jan Juc to Moggs Creek
Surf Coast Walk: A 34 kilometre walk mostly along the coast, starting at the Jan Juc and finishing at Moggs Creek. It can be easily intercepted at Bells Beach, Point Addis, Anglesea, Aireys Inlet and Fairhaven, and be broken up into shorter legs: Jan Juc to Bells Beach (3 km, 1 hour, one way), Bells Beach to Point Addis (5 km, 2 hours, one way), Point Addis to Anglesea (6 km, 2 hours, one way), Anglesea to Aireys Inlet (10 km, 3 hours, one way), and Aireys Inlet to Moggs Creek (10 km, 4 hours, one way).

Point Addis
Ironbark Basin Reserve: Located on the Point Addis Road and accessible from the first carpark half a kilometre from the Great Ocean Road. There are three walks: the Nature Trail (1 km return, including aboriginal references), the Ironbark Track (5 km return) and the Jarosite Track (5 km return, with the first section suitable for wheelchairs and baby strollers)

Anglesea
Coogoorah Park: Located on the western side of the river and accessible from River Reserve Road, comprising a network of short tracks, boardwalks and bridges through bushland and wetland.
Heathland Cliff Walk: Starts at the car park at the end of Purnell Street, a 3.5 kilometre (return) looped walk taking about 40 minutes.

Aireys Inlet
Currawong Falls: Access from the Distillery Creek picnic ground, a 12 kilometre walk (return), taking about 4 hours.
Distillery Creek Nature Trail: Starts at the Distillery Creek picnic ground, an easy 1.75 kilometre walk (return), taking about half an hour.
Ironbark Gorge Walk: Starts at the Distillery Creek picnic ground, an easy 5 kilometre walk (return), taking between 1.5 and 2 hours.

Moggs Creek
Moggs Creek Circuit Walk: Starts at Moggs Creek picnic ground. A 1.5 kilometre walk (return), taking about half an hour.
Ocean View Walk: Starts at Moggs Creek picnic ground. A 4 kilometre walk (return), taking about 1.5 hours.

Pennyroyal
Aquila Falls: Access from Dunses Track, running off Pennyroyal Valley Road. A 3.5 kilometre walk (return), taking about 1 hour.

Lorne
Cora Lynn Cascades: Access from Blanket Leaf picnic ground. A 4 kilometre walk (return), taking 1.5 hours. Or you can continue on past the cascades down Cora Lynn Creek to the Cora Lynn carpark, a 6 kilometre walk (one way), taking 2.5 hours.
Cumberland Falls: Access from Cumberland River Reserve. A 6 kilometre walk (return), following the Cumberland River and taking about 2 hours.
Erskine Falls: Access from Erskine Falls carpark, a 5 minute walk. Also, an 8 kilometre walk (one way) from the falls down the Erskine River takes you all the way back to Lorne, taking 3 to 4 hours.
Erskine Valley Walk: Starts at the Kia-Ora caravan park. A 2 kilometre walk (return) upstream to The Rapids and The Sanctuary taking about 1 hour.

Lorne cont.
Kalimna Falls (Upper and Lower): Access from Sheoak picnic ground. An 8 kilometre walk (return) up the Sheoak Creek, taking 4 hours.
Phantom Falls: Access from Allenvale carpark. A 2.5 kilometre walk (return) up the Saint George River, taking about 1.5 hours.
Phantom Falls – The Canyon – Won Wondah Falls – Henderson Falls: Access from either the Allenvale carpark or the Sheoak picnic ground. A 9 kilometre (return) looped walk, taking about 4 hours.
Sheoak Falls: Access from Sheoak picnic ground. A 7 kilometre walk (return), taking 3 hours. Or they are accessible from the carpark on the Great Ocean Road at the mouth of the Sheoak Creek. A 1 kilometre walk (return), taking about half an hour.

Kennett River
Carisbrook Falls Scenic Reserve: Located 7 km south-west of Kennett River and accessible from the carpark on the Great Ocean Road beside the Carisbrook Creek bridge. A 1 kilometre walk (return), taking about 1 hour.
Grey River Walk: Starts at the third picnic ground along the Grey River Road. A 1 kilometre walk (return), taking about 40 minutes.

Skenes Creek
Sabine Falls: Access from the picnic ground on Sunnyside Road. A 3.5 kilometre (return) looped walk, that is quite hard, taking 1.5 to 2 hours.
Stevenson Falls: Access from the picnic ground at the end of the Upper Gellibrand Road. A 1.5 kilometre walk (return), taking about 1 hour.

Apollo Bay
Beauchamp Falls: Access from the picnic ground on Beauchamp Falls Road. A 2.5 kilometre walk (return) taking about 1 hour.
Hopetoun Falls: Access from the carpark on the Aire Valley Road. A half kilometre walk (return), taking about 45 minutes.
Marriners Falls: Access from the end of Barham Valley Road. A 3 kilometre walk (return) along the Barham River, taking about 45 minutes.
Elliot River Walk: Starts at Shelly Beach carpark. A 4 kilometre walk (return), that is quite hard, taking 2 hours.
Maits Rest Rainforest Track & Boardwalk: Starts at Maits Rest carpark. An 800 metre walk (return), taking about 40 minutes.

Blanket Bay
Blanket Bay – Telegraph Walk: Starts 40 metres north-east of Blanket Bay Creek. A 6 kilometre (return) looped walk, taking 3 hours.
Red Hill Track: Starts at the junction of Red Hill Track and Blanket Bay Road. A 12 kilometre (return) looped walk, taking 5 hours.

Cape Otway
Rainbow Falls: Access from Bimbi Park (private land) on the Otway Lighthouse Road. A 6 kilometre walk (return), taking 3 hours.
Cape Otway to Aire Walk: Starts at Cape Otway Lighthouse or Aire River camping ground. A 11 kilometre walk (one way), taking 4 hours.

Aire River
Escarpment Walk: Starts on the east side of the bridge at the Aire River camping ground. A 4 kilometre walk (return), taking 2 hours.

Johanna
Johanna Falls: Access from Johanna Falls Reserve on Blue Johanna Road. A 20 minute walk (return).

Johanna cont.

Wangerrip Falls: Access from Johanna Falls Reserve on Blue Johanna Road, then over private land. A 40 minute walk (return).

Johanna Beach Walk: Starts at Johanna Beach carpark. An 8 kilometre walk (return) along the beach eastward to Rotten Point then back the same way, taking 3 hours.

Lavers Hill

Beauty Spot Walk: Starts at the Beauty Spot carpark (2.5 km south of Lavers Hill). A 1 kilometre walk (return), taking about 30 minutes.

Triplet Falls: Access from the carpark on Phillips Track. A half kilometre walk (return), taking 20 minutes.

Melba Gully State Park: Located on the Great Ocean Road 3 km west of Lavers Hill. A 1 kilometre (return) looped walk, taking 30 minutes.

Moonlight Head

Wreck Beach Walk: Starts at the first carpark on Moonlight Head Road. A 1.5 kilometre walk (return), taking about 1 hour and quite steep but with steps all the way.

Gable Lookout Walk: Starts at the second carpark at the end of Moonlight Head Road. A 1 kilometre walk (return), taking half an hour.

Princetown

Rivernook Track Walk: Starts at the Princetown Recreation Reserve or Moonlight Head Road. An 11 kilometre walk (one way) along the Old Coach Road, taking 4 hours.

Port Campbell

Loch Ard Gorge Walks: Start at the carparks within the Loch Ard Tourist Precinct. A series of themed walks that are interconnected and link the various attractions. They range from half a kilometre to 3 kilometres (return), taking between 20 minutes and 1.5 hours.

Port Campbell Discovery Walk: Starts at the western end of Port Campbell beach, or the scenic lookout carpark on the Great Ocean Road 1 km west of the bridge. A 5 kilometre walk (return), taking about 1.5 hours.

Peterborough

Bay of Islands Walk: Starts at the Bay of Islands carpark. A 3 kilometre walk (return), taking 2 hours.

Childers Cove

Sandy Bay to Stanhope Bay Walk: Starts at the carpark above Sandy Bay. A 4.5 kilometre (return) looped walk, taking 2.5 hours.

Warrnambool

Hopkins Falls: Access from Hopkins Falls carpark (overlooking the falls) on Hopkins Falls Road.

The Mahogany Walking Track: A 22 kilometre walk between Warrnambool and Port Fairy, that can be easily intercepted at various points including Levy Point carpark, Gormans Road carpark and Killarney beach, and be broken up into shorter legs.

Tower Hill State Game Reserve: Located on the Princes Highway at Tower Hill 4 km east of Killarney. There are two half hour walks, a 45 minute walk, and two that are one hour (some can be combined to create a longer walk).

Port Fairy

Griffiths Island Walk: Starts at the South Passage carpark. A 2 kilometre (return) looped walk, taking 1 hour.

Tyrendarra – Mount Eccles National Park

Crater Rim Nature Walk: Starts from the carpark. A 2 kilometre (return) looped walk, taking one hour.

Lake Walk: Starts from the carpark. A 1.5 kilometre (return) looped walk, taking 45 minutes.

Lava Canal Walk: Starts at the carpark (via the cave). A 6 kilometre walk (return), taking about 2 hours.

Portland

Cape Nelson State Park Sea Cliff Nature Walk: Starts at the carpark near the intersection of Cape Nelson Road and Scenic Road. A 3 kilometre (return) looped walk, taking 2 hours.

Fawthrop Lagoon: Starts at the Botanic Gardens in Cliff Street. A 5 kilometre (return) looped walk, taking about 1.5 hours.

Mount Richmond National Park: Four walks, all starting at the carpark, and all take about 1 hour (return).

Smelter Nature Walk: Starts at the Quarry gates just south of the aluminium smelter. A 4.5 kilometre walk (return), taking about 1.5 hours (suitable for wheelchairs and baby strollers)

The Great South West Walk: A 250 kilometre walk starting at the Portland Tourist Information Centre that leads around Portland Bay then north-west towards Nelson via the Lower Glenelg National Park and along the Glenelg River. From Nelson it returns to Portland following the coastline along Discovery Bay, Bridgewater Bay and Nelson Bay. The track is signposted and there are 16 campsites evenly spaced along the route for the specific use of walkers, each with pit toilet, fireplace and water supply. It is recommended to register your plans at the Portland police station or Nelson Conservation and Natural Resources office before setting out. The walk can be broken up into shorter sections of varying lengths (as short as 2 kilometres). Details of these and the overall walk are described at length in various brochures obtainable from tourist information centres.

Cape Bridgewater

The Blowholes – The Springs – Petrified Forest Walk: Starts at the Blowholes carpark at the end of Blowholes Road. A 4 kilometre walk (return), taking about 1.5 hours. (The Blowholes and Petrified Forest are each only a 5 minute walk from the carpark.)

Nelson – Discovery Bay Coastal Park

Lake Monibeong Walk: Starts at the Lake Monibeong camping ground. A 12 kilometre (return) looped walk taking about 4 hours.

Nelson – Lower Glenelg National Park

Princess Margaret Rose Caves Walk: Starts near the cave entrance. A 6 kilometre (return) walk along the river taking about 2 hours.

Pritchards Walk: Starts at Pritchards camping ground. A 3.5 kilometre walk (return) taking 1.5 hours.

River View Nature Walk: Starts at the Princess Margaret Rose Caves entrance. A short 500 metre (return) looped walk taking about 15 minutes.

Sapling Creek Walk: Starts at Sapling Creek camping ground. A 2.5 kilometre walk (return) taking 1 hour.

DIVING SERVICES

Geelong
Geelong Dive and Outdoor Centre
178 Moorabool Street, Geelong
Tel. 052 213 342

Dive'n'Video
356 Latrobe Terrace, Geelong
Tel. 052 212 460

Southern Cross Divers
92 Pakington Street, West Geelong
Tel. 052 224 899

Queenscliff
Queenscliff Dive Centre
37 Learmonth Street, Queenscliff
Tel. 052 581 188

Apollo Bay
Mobil Bayside Service Station
Great Ocean Road, Apollo Bay
Tel. 052 376 548

Port Campbell
Schomberg Diving Services
Lord Street, Port Campbell
Tel. 055 986 499

Warrnambool
Warrnambool Diving Services
223 Lava Street, Warrnambool
Tel. 055 621 685

Portland
Professional Diving Services
113 Bentinck Street, Portland
Tel. 055 236 392

Scuba Divers Federation of Victoria
13 Notlen Street, Ringwood, Melbourne
Tel. 03 879 2434

GARDENS OPEN TO THE PUBLIC

Queenscliff
Stoneacres Farm
(September to May & nursery)
330 Scotchmans Road,
Drysdale
Tel. 052 593 109

Ocean Grove
Wirruna
(Including nursery)
660 Wallington Road,
Wallington
Tel. 052 501 971

Torquay
Toolangi
(October to May)
625 Nortons Road,
Paraparap
Tel. 052 661 552

Anglesea
Otway Roses
(October to June, & tea-rooms)
450 Wormbete Station Road,
Winchelsea South
Tel. 052 887 382
Tel. 018 526 525

Gellibrand
The Croft Garden
(October to Easter)
Beech Forest Road,
Barongarook
Tel. 052 338 253

Wanawong
(By appointment)
Beech Forest Road,
Burtons Lookout
Tel. 052 338 215

Warrnambool
Fletcher Jones Gardens
Flaxman Street, Warrnambool

Portland
Burswood Homestead
15 Cape Nelson Road, Portland
Tel. 055 234 686

Nelson
Waterfall Gardens
(October to May)
Wanwin Road, Dartmour
Tel. 055 281 253

Botanic Gardens
Geelong – Garden Street
Camperdown – Park Road
Warrnambool – Queen Street
Portland – Cliff Street

GOLF COURSES

Queenscliff Golf Club
Swan Island
Tel. 052 581 951

Point Lonsdale Golf Club
Fellows Road
Tel. 052 581 955

Ocean Grove Golf Club
Guthridge Street
Tel. 052 562 795

Barwon Heads Golf Club
Golf Links Road
Tel. 052 542 302

Torquay Golf Club
Great Ocean Road
Tel. 052 612 005

Anglesea Golf Club
Noble Street
Tel. 052 631 582

Lorne Golf Club
Holiday Street
Tel. 052 891 267

Apollo Bay Golf Club
Nelson Street
Tel. 052 376 474

Peterborough Golf Club
Schomberg Road
Tel. 055 985 245

Warrnambool Golf Club
Younger Street
Tel. 055 622 108

Port Fairy Golf Club
Woodbine Road
Tel. 055 681 654

Portland Golf Club
Victoria Parade
Tel. 055 232 523

HORSE TRAIL RIDES

Ocean Grove
Koombahla Park Equestrian
Centre
365 Wallington Road, Wallington
Tel. 052 551 020

Torquay
Spring Creek Trail Rides
245 Portreath Road,
Bellbrae West
Tel. 052 661 541

Anglesea
Seamist Stud
Gum Flat Road,
Wensleydale
Tel. 052 887 255

Aireys Inlet
Blazing Saddles
Hartleys Road,
Aireys Inlet
Tel. 052 897 149

Apollo Bay
Wild Dog Trails
Wild Dog Road,
Apollo Bay
Tel. 052 376 441

Cape Otway
Bimbi Park
Otway Lighthouse Road,
Cape Otway
Tel. 052 379 246

HORSE TRAIL RIDES Continued

Moonlight Head
Sea Reach Horse Treks
Great Ocean Road
Tel. 052 375 214

Portland
Rundells Riding School
Hodgetts Road, Gorae
Tel. 055 292 303

Nelson
Honeysuckle Stud
Border Road, Caroline
Tel. 087 384 193

MAJOR ANNUAL EVENTS

January
Lorne: Pier to Pub Swim Classic

March
Port Fairy: Folk Music Festival (Labour Day weekend)

Easter
Bells Beach: Rip Curl Easter Surfing Classic

May
Warrnambool: Warrnambool Racing Carnival and Grand Annual Steeplechase

May / June
Lorne: Great Otway Classic (Marathon starting in Geelong and finishing in Lorne, via Apollo Bay.)

October
Port Fairy: Spring Music Festival (Classical music)

October
Warrnambool: Melbourne to Warrnambool Cycling Classic

November
Portland: Admella Surf Boat Marathon

MARKETS

Queenscliff
Last Sunday of the month,
August to May
Located on the foreshore

Point Lonsdale
Second Sunday of the month,
all year
Located at the primary school

Ocean Grove
First Sunday of the month,
all year
Located at Kingston Park

Barwon Heads
Most Sundays in January &
February
Located in Bridge Road

Torquay
First Sunday of the month,
all year
Located at the primary school

Anglesea
Occasionally on Sundays
Located on the riverbank

Apollo Bay
Every Saturday morning,
September to May
Located on the foreshore

Gellibrand
Second Sunday of the month,
all year
Located near the football
ground

Lavers Hill
Last Sunday in January
Located at the school

Port Campbell
Occasionally on Sundays during
Summer holidays and Easter
Located opposite the foreshore

Warrnambool
Every Sunday, all year
Located at the showgrounds.
Last Sunday of the month,
all year, located at the sale yards

Portland
Third Sunday of month, all year
Located at the Angling Club
on the foreshore

MUSEUMS & HISTORICAL SOCIETIES

Geelong

National Wool Museum
Open daily 10am–5pm
26 Moorabool Centre, Geelong
Tel. 052 264 660

Queenscliff

Bellarine Peninsula Railway
(Railway museum and 5 km or
16 km steam train rides)
Open Sundays; Tuesday &
Thursday of school holidays;
Saturdays in January
Queenscliff Railway Station,
Tel. 052 582 069

Fort Queenscliff Museum
(Military museum and guided
tours of the fortress)
Tours daily during school
holidays 11am, 1pm, 3pm;
weekends 1pm, 3pm
King Street, Queenscliff
Tel. 052 580 730

Marine Discovery Centre
(Educational displays of
marine life)
Open daily during school
holidays 10am–4pm
Weeroona Parade, Queenscliff
Tel. 052 583 344

Queenscliff Historical Centre
(Local history)
Open daily 2pm–4pm
Hesse Street, Queenscliff
Tel. 052 582 511

*Queenscliff Maritime Centre &
Museum*
(Maritime history of Port
Phillip Heads)
Open daily during school
holidays 10.30am–4.30 pm;
weekends 1.30pm–4.30pm
Weeroona Parade, Queenscliff
Tel. 052 583 440

Torquay

Torqair Tiger Moth Museum
Open daily 10am–6pm
Blackgate Road, Torquay
Tel. 052 615 100

Torquay cont.

Bellbrae Carriages
(Horse drawn carriages)
Open by appointment
Brushfields Road, Bellbrae
Tel. 052 612 908

Surfworld Museum
(History of surfboard riding)
Open daily 9am–5pm
Surf Coast Plaza, Torquay
Tel. 052 614 606

Anglesea

*Anglesea and District Historical
Society*
(Local history)
Open first Sunday of month and
each Sunday in Jan. 2pm–4pm
5 McMillan Street, Anglesea
Tel. 052 631 430

Lorne

*Babington's Benwerrin Saw Mill
Museum*
(Including saw milling
demonstrations)
Open daily except Friday
10am–4pm mid October–April
Mount Sabine Road, Benwerrin
Tel. 052 891 254

Lorne Historical Society
(Local history)
Open Sundays 1pm–4pm;
Saturdays Sept.–May 1pm–4pm
59 Mountjoy Parade, Lorne
Tel. 052 891 551

Shell Museum
Open daily 9am–4.30pm
1 William Street, Lorne
Tel. 052 891 212

Apollo Bay

Historical Museum
(Local history, also known as
Old Cable Station Museum)
Open daily during school holi-
days 2pm–5pm; weekends
2pm–5pm
Great Ocean Road, Apollo Bay
Tel. 052 376 505
Tel. 052 376 656

Apollo Bay cont.

Bass Strait Shell Museum
Open daily 9.30am–8pm
12 Noel Street, Apollo Bay
Tel. 052 376 395

Princetown

Glenample Homestead
(Includes local history and shipwreck displays)
Open daily during school holidays 10.30am–5pm; weekends
and Monday & Friday
10.30am–5pm
Great Ocean Road,
near Gibson Steps Beach
Tel. 055 988 209

Port Campbell

Loch Ard Shipwreck Museum
Open daily 9.30–5pm
Lord Street, Port Campbell
Tel. 055 986 463

Port Campbell Historical Society
(Local history and craft shop)
Open weekends, Monday &
Wednesday 12–4pm: daily in
January 12–4pm
Lord Street, Port Campbell
Tel. 055 986 390

Warrnambool

Flagstaff Hill Maritime Museum
(Recreation of early Australian
port and village)
Open daily 9am–5pm
Merri Street, Warrnambool
Tel. 055 647 841

History House
(Local history)
Open first Sunday of the month
and each Sunday in January
2pm–4pm
Gilles Street, Warrnambool
Tel. 055 626 940

Time & Tide Museum
(Shells, clocks and musical
instruments)
Open daily 9am–5pm
17 Stanley St., Warrnambool
Tel. 055 624 874

Port Fairy
Cafe Gazette Museum
(Cricket memorabilia)
Open by appointment
46 Sackville Street,
Port Fairy
Tel. 055 682 690

*Port Fairy Historical Society
Museum*
(Local history)
Open daily during school holi-
days 2pm–5pm; weekend &
Wednesday 2pm–5pm
Gipps Street, Port Fairy
Tel. 055 682 682

Portland
Caledonian Inn Museum
(Early settlers display)
Open daily 10am–4pm
Princes Highway,
Bolwarra
Tel. 055 292 266

Cottage in the Gardens
(Restored historic cottage
and displays)
Open Wednesday & Sunday
1.30pm–3.30pm Sept.–May
Portland Botanic Gardens,
Cliff Street, Portland
Tel. 055 231 790

History House
(Local history and genealogical
research centre)
Open daily 10am–12 & 1pm–4pm
Charles Street, Portland
Tel. 055 222 266

*Portland Powerhouse Vintage
Car Museum*
(Veteran and vintage classic
cars and motorbikes)
Open Monday to Friday
1pm–5pm: during school holi-
days and weekends 10am–5pm
Glenelg Street, Portland
Tel. 055 235 795

PICNIC GROUNDS

Queenscliff
• Foreshore opposite Gellibrand
Street BBQ
• Queenscliff Lighthouse BBQ

Point Lonsdale
• Front beach foreshore BBQ

Ocean Grove
• Barwon River foreshore
beside the golf course via
Guthridge Street BBQ
• Main Beach foreshore BBQ
• Kingston Park, Grubb Rd. BBQ
• Ocean Grove Nature Reserve

Barwon Heads
• Barwon River foreshore near
the bridge BBQ

Breamlea
• Cahir Park at the end of
Horwood Drive BBQ

Torquay
• Fishermans Beach
• Front Beach foreshore BBQ
• Taylor Park, opposite
Fishermans Beach BBQ
• Jan Juc Park, Sunset Strip BBQ

Bellbrae
• Bellbrae Reserve, School
Road BBQ

Bells Beach
• Beside the carpark

Point Addis
• Ironbark Basin Reserve on the
Point Addis Road BBQ

Anglesea
• Anglesea River foreshore BBQ
• Coogoorah Park at the end of
River Reserve Road BBQ
• Point Roadknight near the
beach kiosk BBQ

Aireys Inlet
• Distillery Creek Picnic
Ground on Bambra Road BBQ
• Moggs Creek Picnic Reserve
on Boyd Avenue BBQ
• Beside Painkalac Creek
opposite the shops

Lorne
• Blanket Leaf Picnic Ground
off Erskine Road BBQ
• Shelly Beach near the pier BBQ
• Scotchmans Hill at the south
end of the main beach BBQ
• Beside the pool at the end of
Grove Road BBQ
• North Lorne foreshore BBQ
• Sheoak Picnic Ground on
Allenvale Road BBQ
• Teddy's Lookout, George Street

Cumberland River
• Camping ground entrance

Wye River
• Main beach foreshore.
• Foreshore caravan park BBQ
(May to Nov. for non-campers)
• Playground beside the general
store BBQ

Kennett River
• Grey River Road, at the Grey
River bridge 6 km inland and 2
others before it BBQ
• Carisbrook Falls Scenic
Reserve on the Great Ocean
Road BBQ

Skenes Creek
• Beside the Skenes Creek
bridge
• Sabine Falls on Sunnyside
Road BBQ
• Stevenson Falls on Upper
Gellibrand Road BBQ

Apollo Bay
• Main beach foreshore BBQ
• Elliot River Picnic Ground
behind Shelly Beach at the
carpark BBQ
• Paradise Picnic Reserve and
Barham Fernery on Barham
Valley Road BBQ

Beech Forest
• Aire Valley Reserve on the Aire Valley Road BBQ
• Beauchamp Falls on Beauchamp Falls Road BBQ
• Triplet Falls off Phillips Track BBQ

Blanket Bay
• Beside the camping ground on Blanket Bay Road BBQ

Glenaire
• Aire River camping ground on the Hordern Vale Road BBQ

Lavers Hill
• Beauty Spot Picnic Ground, just off the Great Ocean Road, 3 km south of Lavers Hill
• Melba Gully State Park, just off the Great Ocean Road, 3 km west of Lavers Hill BBQ

Princetown
• Beside the old wooden bridge over the Gellibrand River BBQ
• Glenample Homestead near Gibson Steps BBQ

Port Campbell
• Port Campbell Bay foreshore
• Playground beside tennis courts BBQ

Peterborough
• Curdies Inlet foreshore on Irvine Street BBQ

Bay of Islands
• Crofts Bay on the Great Ocean Road, 1 km east of the Bay of Islands BBQ

Childers Cove
• Beside the carpark BBQ

Warrnambool
• Botanic Gardens in Queen St.
• Cannon Hill off Artillery Crescent BBQ
• Hopkins Falls on Hopkins Falls Road BBQ

Warrnambool cont.
• Lake Pertobe Adventure Playground in Pertobe Road BBQ
• Olympic Pool in Queen St. BBQ
• Payne Reserve beside the bridge over the Merri River at Dennington BBQ
• Swan Reserve at the Tourist Information Centre in Raglan Parade BBQ
• The Blue Hole on the eastern side of the Hopkins Rivermouth BBQ

Killarney
• Tower Hill State Game Reserve BBQ
• Beside the camping ground on the foreshore BBQ

Port Fairy
• East Beach at the carpark in Rogers Place BBQ
• Gardens Reserve in the Gardens Caravan Park BBQ
• Martins Point at the southern end of Gipps Street BBQ
• Mills Reserve on the riverbank in Griffiths Street opposite the wharf BBQ

Yambuk
• Lake Yambuk BBQ

Mount Eccles National Park
• Beside camping ground BBQ

Fitzroy Rivermouth
• Beside camping ground BBQ

Narrawong
• Within the camping and recreation reserve BBQ
• Saw Pit Picnic Ground in the Narrawong State Forest BBQ
• Surrey Ridge on Coffeys Lane towards Heathmer BBQ

Portland
• Battery Point at the southern end of Port Road BBQ
• Botanic Gardens in Cliff Street BBQ

Portland cont.
• Fawthrop Lagoon BBQ
• Henty Beach BBQ
• Hanlon Parade Lookout BBQ
• Gardens opposite the hospital in Bentinck St. BBQ
• Lions Club Fauna Reserve in Bridgewater Road BBQ

Cape Nelson State Park
• Scenic Road Picnic Ground BBQ

Cape Bridgewater
• Bridgewater Lakes BBQ
• Bridgewater Beach foreshore

Mount Richmond National Park
• At the carpark BBQ

Discovery Bay Coastal Park
• Swan Lake BBQ
• Lake Monibeong BBQ

Lower Glenelg National Park
There are 9 picnic and camping grounds accessible by car along the Glenelg River in the park, all with BBQ facilities. The largest and most accessible are Princess Margaret Rose Caves and Pritchards.

Nelson
• On the riverbank near the tennis courts BBQ
• On the riverbank near the hotel BBQ
• Simsons Landing on the riverbank 2 km north of Nelson BBQ

RESTAURANTS OF NOTE

Geelong
Cafe Botticelli
111 Pakington Street,
Geelong West
Tel. 052 298 292

Empire Grill
66 McKillop Street, Geelong
Tel. 052 232 132

Fishermen's Pier
Yarra Street, Western Beach,
Geelong
Tel. 052 224 100

Harry's Restaurant
50 Little Malop Street, Geelong
Tel. 052 299 677

Queenscliff
Harry's
Princess Park, Gellibrand Street
Queenscliff
Tel. 052 583 750

Lombardis On Queenscliff
38 Hesse Street, Queenscliff
Tel. 052 583 277

Pasquini's at Suma Park
Bellarine Highway, Marcus Hill
Tel. 052 581 724

The Queenscliff Hotel
16 Gellibrand St., Queenscliff
Tel. 052 581 066

Vue Grand
46 Hesse Street, Queenscliff
Tel. 052 581 544

Ocean Grove
Thai Mekong Restaurant
63a The Terrace, Ocean Grove
Tel. 052 561 161

The Mex
Grubb Road, Ocean Grove
Tel. 052 551 959

Torquay
Ida's By The Sea
28 The Esplanade, Torquay
Tel. 052 612 253

Torquay cont.
Zeally's
35 The Esplanade, Torquay
Tel. 052 613 492

Southern Rose
Great Ocean Road, Torquay
Tel. 052 612 038

Anglesea
Saylers Restaurant
Great Ocean Road, Anglesea
Tel. 052 631 440

Aireys Inlet
McGinty's
Great Ocean Road, Aireys Inlet
Tel. 052 896 996

Birregurra
Sunnybrae
Cape Otway Road, Birregurra
Tel. 052 362 276

Lorne
Kosta's
48 Mountjoy Parade, Lorne
Tel. 052 891 883

Mark's
124 Mountjoy Parade, Lorne
Tel. 052 891 307

Normandy Fare Cafe
Grove Road, Lorne
Tel. 052 891 004

Reif's Restaurant
84 Mountjoy Parade, Lorne
Tel. 052 892 366

The Arab
94 Mountjoy Parade, Lorne
Tel. 052 891 435

Skenes Creek
Chris's Beacon Point Restaurant
Skenes Creek Rd., Skenes Creek
Tel. 052 376 411

Apollo Bay
Beaches Restaurant
Great Ocean Road, Apollo Bay
Tel. 052 376 309

Apollo Bay cont.
Bernie's Restaurant
Great Ocean Road, Wongarra
Tel. 052 370 228

Port Campbell
Emma's
Lord Street, Port Campbell
Tel. 055 986 458

Warrnambool
Bojangles
61 Liebig Street, Warrnambool
Tel. 055 628 751

Childers Licensed Restaurant
525 Raglan Parade,
Warrnambool
Tel. 055 623 866

Clovelly Restaurant
Cnr. Banyan & Merri Streets,
Warrnambool
Tel. 055 611 415

Mahogany Ship
Flagstaff Hill, Warrnambool
Tel. 055 611 833

Port Fairy
Dublin House Inn
57 Bank Street, Port Fairy
Tel. 055 681 822

Lunch
20 Bank Street, Port Fairy
Tel. 055 682 642

Merrijig Inn Restaurant
1 Campbell Street, Port Fairy
Tel. 055 682 324

Portofino By The Sea
28 Bank Street, Port Fairy
Tel. 055 681 047

Portland
Pino's Pizza House
8 Julia Street, Portland
Tel. 055 217 388

Selwyns of Sandilands
33 Percy Street, Portland
Tel. 055 233 319

SCENIC FLIGHTS – AIRCRAFT CHARTER

Geelong
Geelong Air Charter
540 Surf Coast Highway,
Mount Duneed
Tel. 052 641 273

Barwon Heads
South Barwon Air Services
Barwon Heads Rd, Connewarre
Tel. 052 542 338

Bellarine Aviation
PO Box 158, Queenscliff
Tel. 041 8317 648
Tel. 052 584 045

Torquay
Torqair Tiger Moth World
Blackgate Road, Torquay
Tel. 052 615 100

Apollo Bay
Geelong Air Charter
Apollo Bay Airfield, Marengo
Tel. 052 641 273

Great Ocean Road Airtours
Apollo Bay Airfield, Marengo
Tel. 052 615 100

Port Campbell
Bellarine Aviation
(helicopter)
PO Box 158, Queenscliff
Tel. 041 8317 648
Tel. 052 584 045

Helicopter Operators
136 Bromfield Street,
Warrnambool
Tel. 055 627 215

Peterborough
Shipwreck Coast Scenic Flights
Great Ocean Road,
Peterborough
Tel. 055 985 441
Tel. 055 986 369 (bookings)

Warrnambool
Sharp Aviation
Warrnambool Airport, Illowa
Tel. 055 659 222

South West Aviators
Warrnambool Airport, Illowa
Tel. 055 659 348

Portland
Sharp Aviation
Portland Airport, Cashmore
Tel. 055 265 316

SWIMMING POOLS

Geelong
Splashdown Leisure Centre
(Indoor and heated with large
indoor slide)
Coppards Road,
Whittington
Tel. 052 484 555

Leisure Link
(Indoor and heated)
Reynolds Road, Belmont
Tel. 052 439 595

Lorne
Lorne Foreshore Pool
(Outdoor)
Lorne foreshore
Open December to March
Tel. 052 891 382

Otway Homestead
(Indoor and heated)
Erskine Falls Road, Lorne
Tel. 052 891 147

Apollo Bay
Apollo Bay Community Pool
(Outdoor and solar heated)
Costin Street, Apollo Bay
Tel. 052 376 155
Tel. 052 376 483 (the school)

Petticoat Creek Pool
(Indoor and heated)
Great Ocean Road, Petticoat Ck.
Tel. 052 376 825

Lavers Hill
Lavers Hill School
(Indoor and heated)
Great Ocean Road, Lavers Hill
Tel. 052 373 213

Timboon
Timboon Swimming Pool
(Outdoor and solar heated)
Open November to March
Curdievale Road, Timboon
Tel. 055 983 285

Warrnambool
Action Leisure Centre
(Indoor and heated)
3 Mortlake Road,
Warrnambool
Tel. 055 625 050

Figtree Holiday Village
(Indoor and heated)
33 Lava Street,
Warrnambool
Tel. 055 611 233

Warrnambool Olympic Pool
(Outdoor and heated)
Open October to April
Queen Street, Warrnambool
Tel. 055 647 845

Portland
The Place
(Indoor and heated)
Bentinck Street, Portland
Tel. 055 222 259

TOURS & TREKKING – LOCALLY OPERATED

Great Ocean Road
AAA Plus Surf Tours
(Surfboard riding tours)
Tel. 018 521 486

Queenscliff
Queenscliff Historical Tours
(Walking and bus tours)
Tel. 052 583 403

Barwon Heads
Go Canoe – Go Sail
(Canoe and yacht rental,
training and tours)
Tel. 015 342 059

Lorne
Lorne Tours
(Bus tours)
Tel. 052 891 152
Tel. 052 363 363

The Otway Ranges
Adventure Tours 4X4
(4WD camping and trekking)
Tel. 052 439 955

Otway Bush Tours
(4WD camping, bushwalking
and eco tours)
Tel. 052 338 395

Otwild Adventures
(Bushwalking, abseiling and
eco tours)
Tel. 052 891 740

Port Campbell
Port Campbell Shuttle Service
(4WD tours)
Tel. 055 986 369

Warrnambool
Seeall Tours
(Bus tours)
Tel. 055 625 795

Port Fairy
Port Fairy Historic Tours
(Walking tours)
Tel. 055 682 682

Hamilton
Eagle Aboriginal Tours
(Aboriginal cultural tours)
Tel. 055 711 581

Portland
Destination Tour Guides
(Walking and bus tours)
Tel. 055 231 645

Portland Heritage Walks
(Walking tours)
Tel. 055 232 671

South West Adventures
(Canoeing, caving and
mountain bike riding)
Tel. 055 295 305
Tel. 018 527 821

Nelson
South West Canoe Service
(Canoe hire and tours)
Tel. 087 384 141

See also: Boat Charters

UNUSUAL THINGS TO DO

Great Ocean Road
AAA Plus Surf Tours
(Surfboard riding tours)
Point Lonsdale
Tel. 018 521 486

Geelong and Coast Motor
Cycle Tours
(Harley Davidson motorcycle hire)
Highton, Geelong
Tel. 052 433 366
Tel. 1800 633 366

Queenscliff
Bellarine Peninsula Railway
(Steam train rides)
Queenscliff Railway Station
Tel. 052 582 069

Ocean Grove
Bellarine Adventure Golf
(Elaborate mini-golf course)
Bellarine Highway, Wallington
Tel. 052 503 777

Country Connection Trout Farm
(Trout-farm fishing)
Swan Bay Road,
Wallington
Tel. 052 502 756

Torquay
Torqair Tiger Moth World
(Tiger Moth scenic flights)
Blackgate Road, Torquay
Tel. 052 615 100

Anglesea
Anglesea Golf Club
(Golfing with kangaroos)
Noble Street, Anglesea
Tel. 052 631 582

Go Ride A Wave
(Learning to surf)
3 Harvey Street, Anglesea
Tel. 052 632 111

Horsedrawn Holidays
(Gypsy wagons drawn by
clydesdales)
350 Portreath Road, Moriac
Tel. 052 661 612

Lorne
Babington's Benwerrin Saw Mill
Museum
(Timber milling demonstrations)
Mount Sabine Rd, Benwerrin.
Tel. 052 891 254

Gentle Annie Berry Gardens
(Berry picking and trout-farm
fishing)
520 Penny Royal Valley Road,
Deans Marsh
Tel. 052 363 391

Otwild Adventures
(Abseiling)
47 Deans Marsh Road, Lorne
Tel. 052 891 740

UNUSUAL THINGS TO DO Continued

Port Fairy
Hot Glass Studio
(Glass blowing demonstrations)
62 Regent Street, Port Fairy
Tel. 055 682 794

Rosebrook Farm Sheep Shed
(Sheep shearing and sheep dog
demonstrations)
McSweens Road, Rosebrook
Tel. 055 681 667

Nelson
Nelson Boat Hire
(Houseboat river cruising)
Kellett Street, Nelson
Tel. 087 384 048

VINEYARDS

Geelong
Scotchmans Hill Vineyard
Open by appointment
Scotchmans Road, Drysdale
Tel. 052 513 176

Austin Barrabool Wine
Open by appointment
50 Lemins Road, Waurn Ponds
Tel. 052 418 114

Prince Albert Vineyard
Open by appointment
100 Lemins Road, Waurn Ponds
Tel. 052 418 091

Waybourne Winery
Open by appointment
60 Lemins Road, Waurn Ponds
Tel. 052 418 477

Breamlea
The Minya Vineyard & Winery
Open by appointment
Minya Lane,
Connewarre
Tel. 052 641 397

Torquay
Mount Duneed Winery
Open for sales
70 Feehans Road,
Mount Duneed
Tel. 052 641 281

Gellibrand
Barongavale Winery
Open by appointment
East West Road,
Barongarook
Tel. 052 338 324

Portland
Barretts Gorae West Wines
Open for Sales
Nelson Highway, Gorae West
Tel. 055 265 251

Crawford River Winery
Open by appointment
"Crawford", Condah
Tel. 055 782 267

Kingsley Wines
Open for sales
50 Bancroft Street, Portland
Tel. 055 231 864

WILDLIFE PARKS & AQUARIUMS

Queenscliff
Marine Discovery Centre
(Educational displays of
marine life)
Weeroona Parade,
Queenscliff
Tel. 052 583 344

Ocean Grove
Moorfield Wildlife Park
(Kangaroos, koalas, wallabies,
wombats, echidnas, dingoes,
deer, sheep, goats and
native birds)
400 Grubb Road,
Wallington
Tel. 052 501 924

Barwon Heads
Jirrahlinga Koala & Wildlife
Sanctuary
(Emus, kangaroos, koalas, wal-
labies, wombats, echidnas, rep-
tiles, dingoes, and native birds)
Taits Road, Barwon Heads
Tel. 052 542 484

Princetown
Otway Ranges Deer &
Wildlife Park
(Emus, kangaroos, wallabies,
wombats, deer and native birds)
Great Ocean Road, Princetown
Tel. 052 375 262

Warrnambool
Warrnambool Aquarium
Breakwater, Warrnambool
Tel. 055 622 581

Killarney
Tower Hill State Game Reserve
(Emus, kangaroos, wallabies,
koalas, native birds and
water-birds)
Princes Highway, Tower Hill
Tel. 055 659 202

Port Fairy
Port Fairy Aquarium &
Shark Pool
35 Gipps Street, Port Fairy
Tel. 055 681 529

Portland
Lions Club Fauna Park
(Emus, kangaroos, wallabies
and peacocks)
Bridgewater Road,
Portland
Tel. 055 222 200

AIRFIELDS

Geelong
Geelong Airport
Torquay Road, Mount Duneed
Tel. 052 641 273

Queenscliff
Private Airfield
Old St. Leonards Road,
St. Leonards
Tel. 052 571 343

Barwon Heads
South Barwon Air Services
Barwon Heads Road,
Connewarre
Tel. 052 542 338

Torquay
Torqair Tiger Moth World
Blackgate Road, Torquay
Tel. 052 615 100

Colac
Colac Airstrip
Irrewarra
Tel. 052 315 399 Wk.
Tel. 052 346 310 Ah.

Apollo Bay
Apollo Bay Airstrip
Telford Street, Marengo
Tel. 052 376 504
(Shire of Colac – Otway)

Peterborough
Cumming Airstrip
Squirrel Creek, Peterborough
Tel. 055 985 244

Shipwreck Coast Scenic Flights
Airstrip
Great Ocean Road, Peterborough
Tel. 055 985 441

Warrnambool
Warrnambool Aerodrome
Yarpturk Road, Illowa
Tel. 055 659 230

Port Fairy
Port Fairy Airstrip
Griffith Street, Port Fairy
Tel. 055 682 600
(Shire of Moyne)

Portland
Portland Airport
Cashmore
Tel. 055 265 201
Tel. 018 527 165

Nelson
Nelson Aeroplane Company
Portland Road, Nelson
Tel. 087 384 211

AIRLINE RESERVATIONS & CAR RENTAL

Ansett..131300 (Australia wide)
Qantas (domestic) ....131313 (Australia wide)
Qantas (International).....................1800 112 121 (Australia wide, except when in Melbourne 805 0111
and when in Sydney 957 0111)

Gull Airport Service.........................052 224 966 A bus shuttle service operates between Geelong
(45 McKillop Street) and Melbourne Airport eleven times daily.

Avis ....1800 225 533 (Australia wide, except when in Sydney 353 9000)
Budget..132727 (Australia wide)
Hertz...131918 (Australia wide)
Thrifty ....1800 226 434 (Australia wide, except when in Sydney 380 5399)

Budget, Hertz and Thrifty all have depots in Warrnambool, should you want to drop the car off and
catch the train back to Melbourne. These three also have depots in Geelong.

AUTOGAS

Ocean Grove
Lofty's Service Station
48 Wallington Road
Tel. 052 561 036

Barwon Heads
Apco Easy Shop
41 Geelong Road
Tel. 052 543 313

Torquay
Surf Coast Auto
108 Geelong Road
Tel. 052 612 002

Lorne
Shell Surfside
70 Mountjoy Parade
Tel. 052 892 593

Apollo Bay
Mobil Bayside Service Station
177 Great Ocean Road
Tel. 052 376 548

Port Campbell
Port Campbell Motors
Lord Street
Tel. 055 986 351

AUTOGAS Continued

Warrnambool
Mobil Central (open 24 hours)
595 Raglan Parade
Tel. 055 612 006

Port Fairy
Alexanders Shell Depot
203 Princes Highway
Tel. 055 681 723

Portland
BP Seaport Service Station
6 Gawler Street
Tel. 055 232 808

BOAT RAMPS

Queenscliff
Located in Swan Bay 300 metres west of fishing fleet wharf.

Ocean Grove
Located near Ocean Grove golf course (via Guthridge Street) providing access to the Barwon River.

Barwon Heads
The first ramp is next to the bridge over the Barwon River (north side), there are two more located further upstream off River Parade. All provide access to the ocean.

Torquay
Located at Fishermans Beach.

Anglesea
Located at Point Roadknight.

Aireys Inlet
Located in the estuary at the lighthouse end, but does not provide access to the ocean. There is an 8 kmh speed limit for boats.

Eastern View
Located 300 metres west of Spout Creek, but not in very good condition.

Lorne
Located beside the pier, smaller craft can be launched from the beach near the foreshore swimming pool.

Apollo Bay
Located between the breakwater and jetty.

Blanket Bay
There is no actual boat ramp here, but access to the beach by vehicles is permitted strictly for the purpose of launching light craft. Point of access to the beach is just before the camping area.

Princetown
Located beside the old wooden bridge (on the way to the Recreation Reserve), providing access to the Gellibrand River and estuary only.

Port Campbell
Light craft can be dragged across the beach (but not driven) into the bay via a ramp beside the Surf Life Saving Clubhouse. The crane on the jetty provides the only other access, but you must be a member of the Port Campbell Boating Club to use it, (see page 127).

Peterborough
The ramp providing access to the sea is located near the eastern end of the golf course, but favours lighter craft and a high tide, as sand coverage is often a problem. A second ramp is located on the western side of the Curdies Inlet 200 metres north of the bridge, providing access to Curdies Inlet only.

Bay Of Islands
Located 500 metres north of the Bay Of Islands carpark. It is very steep and long, usable with 4WD only.

Warrnambool
Located beside the breakwater in Lady Bay.

Killarney
Located at the eastern end of the beach.

Port Fairy
Located in the Moyne River harbour on the eastern side, opposite the fisherman's co-operative.

Yambuk
Located on the eastern side of the Lake Yambuk, near the camping ground, but does not provide access to the ocean.

Tyrendarra East
Located on the Fitzroy River near the river mouth and before the camping ground, but does not provide access to the ocean.

Portland
Located on the western side of the harbour, at the end of Julia Street.

Cape Bridgewater
Located beside the Surf Life Saving Clubhouse.

Nelson
There are two ramps in the town centre providing access to the Glenelg River but not the ocean. One is next to the kiosk, the other is directly opposite, on the other side of the river.

Details of additional camping grounds in Coastal, State and National Parks can be found on page 123

Queenscliff
Beacon Resort (cabins)
78 Bellarine Highway,
Queenscliff
Tel. 052 581 133

Four Winds Caravan Park
(cabins)
40 Bellarine Highway,
Queenscliff
Tel. 052 581 884

Recreation Reserve Camping
Area
Mercer Street, Queenscliff
Tel. 052 581 765

The Springs Caravan Park
(cabins)
54 Bellarine Highway,
Queenscliff
Tel. 052 581 895

Victoria Park
King Street, Queenscliff
Tel. 052 581 765

Point Lonsdale
Golightly Caravan Park
Bowen Road,
Point Lonsdale
Tel. 052 581 765

Royal Caravan Park
Point Lonsdale Road,
Point Lonsdale
Tel. 052 581 765

Spring Hill Holiday Park
84 Bellarine Highway,
Point Lonsdale
Tel. 052 582 425

Ocean Grove
Collendina Caravan Park
(cabins)
177 Bonnyvale Road,
Ocean Grove
Tel. 052 551 966

Ocean Grove cont.
Green Valley Caravan Park
(cabins)
14 The Terrace,
Ocean Grove
Tel. 052 551 605

Ocean Grove Caravan Park
(cabins)
90 Wallington Road,
Ocean Grove
Tel. 052 562 233

Riverview Family Caravan Park
(includes foreshore camping
reserve)
Sweetman Parade,
Ocean Grove
Tel. 052 561 600

Ti-Tree Village Caravan Park
(cabins)
34 Orton Street,
Ocean Grove
Tel. 052 554 433

Wynndean Holiday Resort
15 The Esplanade,
Ocean Grove
Tel. 052 551 766

Barwon Heads
Barwon Heads Foreshore
Caravan Park (cabins)
Ewing Blyth Drive,
Barwon Heads
Tel. 052 542 572

Rondor Caravan Park (cabins)
Sheepwash Road,
Barwon Heads
Tel. 052 542 753

Breamlea
Breamlea Caravan Park (cabins)
Horwood Drive,
Breamlea
Tel. 052 641 352

Torquay
Bernell Tourist Caravan Park
(cabins)
55 Geelong Road, Torquay
Tel. 052 612 493

Torquay cont.
Jan Juc Caravan Park (cabins)
Sunset Strip, Jan Juc
Tel. 052 612 932

Torquay Public Reserves
(cabins)
Bell Street, Torquay
Tel. 052 612 496

Zealley Bay Caravan Park
(cabins)
Cnr Darian Road & Esplanade
Torquay
Tel. 052 612 400

Anglesea
Anglesea Family Caravan Park
(cabins)
Cameron Road, Anglesea
Tel. 052 631 583

Driftwood Caravan Park
(cabins)
Murray Street, Anglesea
Tel. 052 631 640

Narambi Caravan Park (cabins)
11 Camp Road, Anglesea
Tel. 052 631 362

Aireys Inlet
Aireys Inlet Caravan Park
(cabins)
19 Great Ocean Road,
Aireys Inlet
Tel. 052 896 230

Lorne
Babingtons Family Park (cabins)
19 Colac Road, Lorne
Tel. 052 891 760

Lorne Foreshore Reserve
(cabins)
There are 5 camping sites oper-
ated by the Lorne Foreshore
Committee:
•Erskine River (Great Ocean Rd)
•Kia-ora (GOR)
•Top Bank (GOR)
•Ocean Road (GOR)
•Queens Park (Armitage St.)
Tel. 052 891 382

Cumberland River
Cumberland River Caravan
Park (cabins)
Great Ocean Road,
Cumberland River
Tel. 052 891 382

Wye River
Wye River Foreshore
Caravan Park
Great Ocean Road, Wye River
Tel. 052 890 412

Wye River Valley Caravan Park
(cabins)
Great Ocean Road, Wye River
Tel. 052 890 241

Kennett River
Kennett River Camping
Reserve
Great Ocean Road,
Kennett River
Tel. 052 890 272

Skenes Creek
Skenes Creek Camping Reserve
Great Ocean Road,
Skenes Creek
Tel. 052 376 132

Apollo Bay
Kooringal Caravan Park
(cabins)
27 Cawood Street, Apollo Bay
Tel. 052 377 111

Marengo Camping Reserve
Marengo Crescent,
Apollo Bay
Tel. 052 376 813

Pisces Caravan Resort (cabins)
Great Ocean Road, Apollo Bay
Tel. 052 376 749

Recreation Reserve Caravan &
Camp Park
Great Ocean Road, Apollo Bay
Tel. 052 376 577

Waratah Caravan Park (cabins)
7 Noel Street, Apollo Bay
Tel. 052 376 562

Blanket Bay
Otway National Park Camping
Ground
Blanket Bay Road, Blanket Bay
see page 123

Cape Otway
Bimbi Park
Otway Lighthouse Road,
Cape Otway
Tel. 052 379 246

Aire River
Otway National Park Camping
Ground
Hordern Vale Road,
Hordern Vale
see page 123

Johanna
Otway National Park Camping
Ground
Johanna Road, Johanna
see page 123

Lavers Hill
Lavers Hill Roadhouse Caravan
Park (cabins)
Great Ocean Road,
Lavers Hill
Tel. 052 373 251

Princetown
Apostles Camping Park
Princetown
Tel. 055 988 119

Princetown Recreation Reserve
Old Coach Road, Princetown
Tel. 055 988 119
see page 123

Port Campbell
Port Campbell Caravan Park
(cabins)
Tregea Street, Port Campbell
Tel. 055 986 369

Peterborough
Peterborough Coastal
Caravan Park
McGillivray Road,
Peterborough
Tel. 055 985 294

Peterborough cont.
Great Ocean Road Tourist Park
(cabins)
Great Ocean Road,
Peterborough
Tel. 055 985 477

Warrnambool
Caravarna Lodge Caravan Park
(cabins)
81 Henna Street, Warrnambool
Tel. 055 623 376

Figtree Holiday Village (cabins)
33 Lava Street, Warrnambool
Tel. 055 611 233

Flying Horse Inn Caravan Park
(cabins)
Princes Highway, Warrnambool
Tel. 055 624 837

Jubilee Park
Jubilee Park Road, Allansford
Tel. 055 651 327

Ocean Beach Holiday Village
(cabins)
Pertobe Road, Warrnambool
Tel. 055 614 222

Shipwreck Bay Holiday Park
Pertobe Road, Warrnambool
Tel. 055 612 622

Surfside Holiday Park (cabins)
Pertobe Road, Warrnambool
Tel. 055 612 611

Warrnambool Holiday Park
(cabins)
Raglan Parade, Warrnambool
Tel. 055 625 031

Killarney
Killarney Beach Camping Ground
Survey Road, Killarney
Tel. 055 682 600

Port Fairy
Belfast Cove Caravan Park
(cabins)
139 Princes Highway, Port Fairy
Tel. 055 681 816

CARAVAN PARKS & CAMPING GROUNDS Continued

Port Fairy cont.
Catalina Caravan Park (cabins)
Princes Highway, Port Fairy
Tel. 055 681 608

Gardens Reserve Caravan Park
(cabins)
111 Griffith Street, Port Fairy
Tel. 055 681 060

Gum Tree Caravan Park
(cabins)
Toolong Road, Port Fairy
Tel. 055 681 816

Learnean Anchorage Holiday
Park (cabins)
115 Princes Highway, Port Fairy
Tel. 055 681 145

Southcombe Park Caravan Park
James Street, Port Fairy
Tel. 055 682 677

Yambuk
Yambuk Lake Camping Ground
Yambuk Lake Road, Yambuk
Tel. 055 682 600

Tyrendarra East
Fitzroy Rivermouth Camping
Ground
Thompsons Road,
Tyrendarra East
Tel. 055 233 232

Narrawong
Narrawong Caravan Park
(cabins)
Princes Highway, Narrawong
Tel. 055 295 282

Portland
Centenary Caravan Park
(cabins)
184 Bentinck Street,
Portland
Tel. 055 231 487

Claremont Holiday Village
(cabins)
61 Julia Street, Portland
Tel. 055 217 567

Dutton Way Caravan Park
Dutton Way, Portland
Tel. 055 231 904

Henty Bay Caravan Park (cabins)
Dutton Way, Portland
Tel. 055 233 716

Portland Haven Caravan Park
(cabins)
76a Garden Street, Portland
Tel. 055 231 768

Portland Village (cabins)
74 Garden Street, Portland
Tel. 055 235 673

Cape Bridgewater
Cape Bridgewater Caravan
Park (cabins)
Blowholes Road,
Cape Bridgewater
Tel. 055 267 267

Nelson
Nelson Kywong Caravan Park
North Nelson Road, Nelson
Tel. 087 384 174

River Vu Caravan Park (cabins)
Kellett Street, Nelson
Tel. 087 384 123

COMMUNITY HEALTH & MEDICAL CENTRES

When a health centre does not
include a medical clinic, or a
town is not listed below, it is
best to contact the local hospital (page 120) for the address of
a local medical clinic.

Point Lonsdale
Bellarine Peninsula Community
Health Service
(includes medical clinic)
Nelson Road, Point Lonsdale
Tel. 052 581 944

Ocean Grove
Ocean Grove Community
Health Centre
Presidents Ave, Ocean Grove
Tel. 052 561 510

Torquay
Torquay Surf Coast Community
Service
(includes medical clinic)
Bell Street, Torquay
Tel. 052 613 001

Anglesea
Anglesea Surf Coast
Community Service
(includes medical clinic)
McMillan Street, Anglesea
Tel. 052 631 952

Lorne
Lorne Community Health Service
(includes medical clinic)
Albert Street, Lorne
Tel. 052 891 508

Apollo Bay
Apollo Bay Community Health
Service
McLachlan Street,
Apollo Bay
Tel. 052 376 994

Port Campbell
Timboon Community Health
Centre
(includes medical clinic)
Wark Street, Timboon
Tel. 055 983 049

Portland
Portland And District
Community Health Centre
Otway Street, Portland
Tel. 055 234 000

DEPARTMENT OF CONSERVATION & NATURAL RESOURCES

The department is divided into four areas of management:
• National Parks Service
• Forest Service
• Flora, Fauna & Fisheries Service
• Catchment & Land Management Service

Staffing in each office varies according to its size and the local requirements. Work centres are usually staffed by field workers.

PORT PHILLIP AREA
Area Office
205 Thomas Street
Dandenong, Melbourne
Tel. 03 706 7000

Geelong Office
State Public Offices
Cnr Little Malop & Fenwick Sts.
Geelong
Tel. 052 264 667

SOUTH WEST AREA
Area Office
State Public Offices
Cnr Mair & Doveton Streets,
Ballarat
Tel. 053 336 78

Colac Office
83 Gellibrand Street, Colac
Tel. 052 335 533
Anglesea Work Centre
Elizabeth Street
Tel. 052 633 144
Lorne Work Centre
86 Polwarth Road
Tel. 052 891 732
Apollo Bay Work Centre
Cnr Cartwright & Nelson Sts.
Tel. 052 376 889
Forrest Work Centre
Grant Street
Tel. 052 366 204
Gellibrand Work Centre
Charleys Creek Road
Tel. 052 358 201

Lavers Hill Work Centre
Chapplevale-Lavers Hill Rd.
Tel. 052 373 243
Port Campbell Work Centre
Tregea Street
Tel. 055 986 382

Warrnambool Office
214 Koroit Street,
Warrnambool
Tel. 055 624 577

Portland Office
8 Julia Street,
Portland
Tel. 055 233 232
Tower Hill Work Centre
Princes Highway
Tel. 055 659 202
Macarthur Work Centre
Huntly Street
Tel. 055 761 014
Nelson Work Centre
Forest Road
Tel. 087 384 051

DOG KENNELS

Barwon Heads
Jirrahlinga All Pets Boarding
Taits Road, Barwon Heads
Tel. 052 542 484

Ocean Grove
Tsu Lin Boarding Kennels
295 Banks Road, Mannerim
Tel. 052 512 924

Torquay
Addiscott Boarding Kennels
Addiscott Road, Bellbrae
Tel. 052 612 726

Warrnambool
Grassmere Boarding Kennels
'Six Acres', Grassmere
Tel. 055 654 266

Port Fairy
Killarney Kennels
Princes Highway, Killarney
Tel. 055 687 280

DOGS ON BEACHES

More often than not dogs are allowed on the beaches along this coastline. Any restrictions fall into two categories; the first are summer restrictions on town beaches, detailed below, and the second is prohibition in National Parks. In Victoria all dogs over six months old are required to be registered, and when on a beach must be under effective control. This means either they are responsive to verbal command or, if not, must be on a leash. It would pay to keep an eye open for signposts controlling any areas not listed below or for any changes introduced. Unless hours are specified a restriction applies 24 hours a day.

Queenscliff to Point Lonsdale
December 1 – February 28
not allowed on any beaches
between 8 am & 8 pm (except
the beach at Logs carpark).

Ocean Grove
November 1 – April 30
not allowed between Barwon
Rivermouth and Hodgson St.

Barwon Heads
December 1 – April 30
not allowed between the jetty
and the Bluff.

Breamlea
December 1 – April 30
not allowed on Bancoora beach.

Torquay to Jan Juc
December 1 – April 30
not allowed on the beach
between Darian Road, Torquay
and Domain Road, Jan Juc.

Anglesea
December 1 – April 30
not allowed on the beach
between Ramsay Street,
Anglesea and Melba Parade,
Point Roadknight.

Aireys Inlet
December 1 – April 30
not allowed on the beach for a
stretch of 200 metres, west of
Painkalac Creek.

Fairhaven
December 1 – April 30
not allowed in front of Surf Life
Saving Clubhouse.

Moggs Creek
December 1 – April 30
not allowed in front of Moggs
Creek.

Eastern View
December 1 – April 30
not allowed in front of Spout
Creek.

Lorne
December 1 – April 30
not allowed in the Surf Life
Saving Clubhouse area.

December 1 – April 30
not allowed on the remaining
beach up to Little Stony Creek
between 9 am & 7 pm.

Angahook Lorne State Park
Except in the case of the camping grounds, dogs are allowed in
this state park throughout the
year, but must be on a leash.
This includes any beaches

Angahook Lorne State Pk. cont.
within the park, namely those
along the stretch of coastline
between the Cumberland River
and Cape Patton, however the
main beaches at Kennett River
and Wye River are under the
control of foreshore authorities,
see below.

Wye River
December 1 – March 31
not allowed on the main beach.

Kennett River
December 1 – March 31
not allowed on the main beach.

Skenes Creek
December 1 – March 31
not allowed on the main beach.

Apollo Bay
December 1 – March 31
not allowed on the main beach.

**Otway National Park &
Port Campbell National Park**
Dogs are prohibited at all times
from these parks, including the
beaches. Together the two
parks cover a continuous stretch
of coastline that starts at Shelly
Beach (just west of Apollo Bay)
and finishes at Curdies Inlet at
Peterborough. The only exception is Johanna Beach, in which
case dogs are allowed but must
be on a leash.

Peterborough
Not allowed throughout the
year on the rivermouth beach.

Childers Cove
Not allowed throughout
the year.

Warrnambool
November 1 – April 30
not allowed on the main city
beaches.
(Not allowed throughout the
year at the Hopkins Rivermouth)

Port Fairy
December 1 – April 30
not allowed on the beaches
within the urban area between
8am & 8pm

Narrawong
Not allowed throughout the
year on the stretch of beach
beside the caravan park.

Portland
Not allowed throughout the
year between Fishermans
Wharf and the lighthouse
(i.e. Henty Beach and Nun's
Beach), except between dawn
and 8.30 am on Nun's Beach.

Cape Nelson State Park
Not allowed throughout
the year.

Bridgewater Bay
Restrictions for the summer
period are pending.

Discovery Bay Coastal Park
Not allowed throughout the
year, except for a limited area
at Nelson near the ocean beach
carpark, and then only on
a leash.

Nelson
Not allowed on the estuary
river-beach throughout the
year, except for a limited area
near the ocean beach carpark,
and then only on a leash.

FERRY SERVICES – PORT PHILLIP BAY

Peninsula Sea Road Transport
Larkin Parade, Queenscliff
Tel. 052 583 244
All year round vehicle and pas-
senger service.

Sorrento Ferry Service
3433 Nepean Highway, Sorrento
Tel. 059 841 602
Summer till Easter and school
holidays, passenger only service.

FORESHORE COMMITTEES OF MANAGEMENT

Generally, the Department of Conservation and Natural Resources (C&NR) supervises the management of the coastline, however in many areas responsibility has been delegated to either foreshore
committees or the local shire. In the case of coastal, state and national parks, C&NR have direct control.

**Ocean Grove Foreshore
Committee**
From Collendina to
Ocean Grove
Tel. 052 561 600

**Barwon Heads Foreshore
Committee**
From Barwon Heads to
Black Rock
Tel. 052 542 572

Torquay Foreshore Committee
From Point Impossible to
Jan Juc
Tel. 052 612 496

Bells Beach Surfing Reserve
Bells Beach area
Tel. 052 614 202

Anglesea Foreshore Committee
From Point Addis to
Urqhuarts Bluff
Tel. 052 631 583

**Aireys Inlet Foreshore
Committee**
From Urquharts Bluff to
Aireys Inlet
Tel. 03 807 2077

**Fairhaven Foreshore
Committee**
From Aireys Inlet to Grassy Ck.
Tel. 052 896 698

Lorne Foreshore Committee
From North Lorne to
Cumberland River
Tel. 052 891 382

**Wye River Foreshore
Committee**
Wye River
Tel. 052 890 292

**Apollo Bay – Kennett River
Foreshore Committee**
From Kennett River to
Marengo
Tel. 052 366 304

**Bridgewater Foreshore
Committee**
Bridgewater Beach
Tel. 055 233 232

**Nelson Foreshore
Committee**
Nelson
Tel. 087 384 051

HOLIDAY HOUSE ACCOMMODATION – REAL ESTATE AGENTS

Most towns have large numbers of privately owned houses on the market for holiday rental. Some are
available throughout the year, but most are for rent during the summer holidays only. In particular Point
Lonsdale, Ocean Grove, Torquay, Anglesea, Lorne and Apollo Bay have huge listings. Usually real
estate agents handle bookings though in the case of Warrnambool and Portland, the tourist information
centres are more appropriate.

Queenscliff
Jens-Gaunt Real Estate
Tel. 052 583 633

Point Lonsdale
Butler & King
Tel. 052 581 811

J. T. Kerley
Tel. 052 584 100

Ocean Grove
C. J. Keane & Co.
Tel. 052 551 222

Guyett Real Estate
Tel. 052 551 422

Phillip Butlers First National
Tel. 052 551 000

Stockdale & Leggo
Tel. 052 551 380

Wilson McKewan
Tel. 052 561 644

Barwon Heads
Bodey's Real Estate
Tel. 052 543 100

Torquay
C. J. Keane & Co
Tel. 052 614 001

G. R. McCartney & Son
Tel. 052 612 104

Hayden Real Estate
Tel. 052 612 101

L. J. Hooker
Tel. 052 612 121

Torquay Realty
Tel. 052 615 088

Anglesea
Geoff Lewtas Real Estate
Tel. 052 632 214

Hayden Real Estate
Tel. 052 632 133

Ken Smyth
Tel. 052 632 477

Aireys Inlet
L. J. Hooker
Tel. 052 896 261

Lorne
Lorne Real Estate
Tel. 052 891 214

Ken Smyth
Tel. 052 891 278

Apollo Bay
C. J. Keane & Co.
Tel. 052 376 322

Thomas Joyce Sears
Tel. 052 376 258

**Port Campbell &
Peterborough**
Dalgetty Farmers
Tel. 055 983 050

Elders Real Estate
Tel. 055 983 008

Warrnambool
Tourist Information Centre
Tel. 055 647 837

Port Fairy
Colin Robertson
Tel. 055 681 904

Kevin Chiller & Associates
Tel. 055 681 066

Portland
Tourist Information Centre
Tel. 055 232 671
Tel. 1800 035 567

Nelson
Hedditch Real Estate
Tel. 087 384 085

HOSPITALS

Geelong
Geelong Hospital
Ryrie Street, Geelong
Tel. 052 267 111

Colac
Colac District Hospital
Corangamite Street, Colac
Tel. 052 315 111

Lorne
Lorne Community Hospital
Albert Street, Lorne
Tel. 052 891 508

Apollo Bay
Apollo Bay & District
Memorial Hospital
McLachlan Street, Apollo Bay
Tel. 052 376 303

Port Campbell
Timboon & District Hospital
Hospital Road, Timboon
Tel. 055 983 000

Warrnambool
Warrnambool & District
Base Hospital
Ryot Street, Warrnambool
Tel. 055 649 400

Port Fairy
Port Fairy Hospital
Villiers Street, Port Fairy
Tel. 055 681 303

Portland
Portland and District Hospital
Bentinck Street, Portland
Tel. 055 210 333

HOST FARMS

Host farms are a collection of B&B's, homesteads, cottages and cabins that offer accommodation in a rural setting, with the opportunity to experience, or even participate, in farming life. The majority offer self-contained accommodation and all those listed are members of Host Farms Association Inc. 230 Collins Street, Melbourne. Tel. 03 650 2922

Queenscliff
Balla-Wein
Bellarine
Tel. 052 592 232

Torquay
Freshwater Creek Cottages
Freshwater Creek
Tel. 052 645 296

Torquay Country Retreat
Torquay
Tel. 052 613 144

Wendouree Alpaca Stud
Moriac
Tel. 052 661 484

Woodstock
Freshwater Creek
Tel. 052 645 281

Aireys Inlet
The Glen
Aireys Inlet
Tel. 052 896 306

Lorne
Jinda Park
Bambra
Tel. 03 457 5413

Woodhouselee
Bambra
Tel. 052 363 252

Colac – Camperdown
Gannawarra
Birregurra
Tel. 052 362 131

Monnowe Park
Colac
Tel. 052 366 435

Mooleric
Birregurra
Tel. 052 889 214

Colac – Camperdown cont.
Rockbank
Derrinallum
Tel. 055 976 626

Skenes Creek
Barramunga Cabins
Barramunga
Tel. 052 363 302

Apollo Bay
Arcady Homestead
Apollo Bay
Tel. 052 376 493

Seafarers
Apollo Bay
Tel. 052 376 507

Cape Otway
Cape Otway Cottage
Cape Otway
Tel. 052 379 263

Johanna
Johanna Seaside Farm
Johanna
Tel. 052 374 242

Lavers Hill
Laurall Park
Kennedys Creek
Tel. 052 383 213

Princetown
Glenample
Princetown
Tel. 055 988 237

Kangaroobie
Princetown
Tel. 055 988 151

Macka's Farm
Princetown
Tel. 055 988 261

Port Campbell
Boorook Cottage
Timboon – Port Campbell
Tel. 055 987 321

Curdie's Holiday Farm
Timboon
Tel. 055 983 260

Inglenook Cottage
Timboon
Tel. 055 983 250

Renyard's Farm Holidays
Timboon
Tel. 055 983 152

Warrnambool
Kintyre
Hawkesdale
Tel. 055 608 541

Mount Pleasant
Allansford
Tel. 055 651 266

Red Rattler Train Carriage
Terang
Tel. 055 925 246

Port Fairy
Taroona
Macarthur
Tel. 055 784 235

Portland
Burswood Homestead
Portland
Tel. 055 234 686

Quamby Park
Tyrendarra
Tel. 055 295 280

HOSTEL & BACKPACKERS ACCOMMODATION

Anyone can stay at these places, but Youth Hostels Association members will pay at a lesser rate at YHA member accommodation. The YHA Victorian headquarters are in Melbourne
Tel. 03 670 3802

Geelong
Geelong YHA Hostel
1 Lonsdale Street, Geelong
Tel. 052 216 583

Queenscliff
Queenscliff Inn
59 Hesse Street, Queenscliff
Tel. 052 583 737

Lorne
Great Ocean Road Backpackers
(associate member of YHA)
10 Erskine Avenue, Lorne
Tel. 052 891 809

Apollo Bay
Pisces Caravan Resort
Ocean Road, Apollo Bay
Tel. 052 376 749

Lavers Hill
Lavers Hill Roadhouse &
Caravan Park
Great Ocean Road, Lavers Hill
Tel. 052 373 251

Cape Otway
Bimbi Park
Otway Lighthouse Road,
Cape Otway
Tel. 052 379 246

Princetown
Apostles Camping Park
Princetown
Tel. 055 988 119

Port Campbell
Port Campbell Hostel
18 Tregea Street, Port Campbell
Tel. 055 986 379

Warrnambool
Surf-Side One Caravan Park
Pertobe Road, Warrnambool
Tel. 055 612 611

Port Fairy
'Emoh' YHA Hostel
8 Cox Street, Port Fairy
Tel. 055 682 468

Portland
Centenary Caravan Park
184 Bentinck Street, Portland
Tel. 055 231 487

'Nioka Farm' Home Hostel
Nelson Road, Mount Richmond
Tel. 055 202 233

LOCAL GOVERNMENT & PORT AUTHORITIES

Borough of Queenscliffe
(Queenscliff and most of
Point Lonsdale)
50 Learmonth Street,
Queenscliff, 3225
Tel. 052 581 377

City of Greater Geelong
(Point Lonsdale to Breamlea)
City Hall, Gheringhap Street,
Geelong, 3220
Tel. 052 270 270

Surf Coast Shire
(Torquay to Cumberland River)
25 Grossmans Road,
Torquay, 3228
Tel. 052 614 202

Shire of Colac – Otway
(Wye River to Cape Volney)
2–6 Rae Street,
Colac, 3250
Tel. 052 315 133

Shire of Corangamite
(Moonlight Head to
Curdies Inlet)
49 Ferguson Street,
Camperdown, 3260
Tel. 055 933 102

Shire of Moyne
(Peterborough to Codrington)
12 Cox Street,
Port Fairy, 3284
Tel. 055 682 600

City of Warrnambool
(Warrnambool)
25 Liebig Street,
Warrnambool, 3280
Tel. 055 647 800

Shire of Glenelg
(Tyrendarra East to Nelson)
Cliff Street,
Portland, 3305
Tel. 055 222 200

Port of Geelong
65 Brougham Street, Geelong
Tel. 052 221 644
•Queenscliff depot
Tel. 052 581 947
•Apollo Bay depot
Tel. 052 376 614

Port of Portland
Barton Place, Portland
Tel. 055 250 900
•Port Fairy depot
Tel. 055 681 108

No pets are allowed when camping in the parks listed below, the only exception is Johanna Beach, in which case dogs are allowed but must be on a leash.

Angahook Lorne State Park
There are five main sites available for camping:
Allenvale
Hammonds Road
Jamieson Track
Sharps Track
Wye River Road
• No toilets
• Take water
• No fires (whatever time of year)
• Inaccessible to caravans
• Enquiries tel. 052 891 732

Otway National Park
Blanket Bay
• 16 sites
(plus campsite for hikers only)
• Toilets
• Take Water
(or obtainable from Parker River and Blanket Bay Creek)
• Unsuitable for caravans
• Fires in fireplaces only
• Enquiries tel. 052 376 889

Parker Hill & Point Franklin
• (accessible via Blanket Bay Rd)
• 10 sites each (approx.)
• No toilets
• Take water
• Unsuitable for caravans
• Fires not allowed

Aire River
• Toilets
• Water available
• Fires in fireplaces only on the eastern site
• Fires only in 30 cm trench, and clear for 3 metres around, on the western site
• Enquiries tel. 052 376 889

Otway National Park cont.
Johanna Beach
• Toilets
• Water available
• Fires only in 30 cm trench, and clear for 3 metres around
• Enquiries tel. 052 376 889

Princetown Recreation Reserve
• located on crown land abutting the national park
• Toilets
• Water available
• Fires only in 30 cm trench, and clear for 3 metres around
• Sites booked on tel. 055 988 119

Port Campbell National Park
Port Campbell Caravan Park
• All facilities including cabins
• Sites booked on tel. 055 986 369

Mount Eccles National Park
Mount Eccles Camping Ground
• Showers
• Toilets
• Water available
• Fires in fireplaces only
• Sites booked on tel. 055 761 014

Discovery Bay Coastal Park
Swan Lake Camp
• 20 sites
• Toilets
• Water available
• Fires in fireplaces only
• Permit required tel. 087 384 051

Lake Monibeong Camp
• 10 sites
• Toilets
• Water available
• Fires in fireplaces only
• Permit required tel. 087 384 051

White Sands Camp
• Clearing for walkers only
• Toilets
• Water available
• Fires in fireplaces only

Lower Glenelg National Park
There are 18 campsites along the Glenelg River in the national park. Half are accessible only by walking track or canoe, the remainder by vehicle and two of which have caravan sites. All the camps have fireplaces, water and toilets. Permits are required and fees payable for the vehicle based camps (tel. 087 384 051), each having between two and four sites (except the larger Princess Margaret Rose Caves and Pritchards sites, see below). The walking and canoe based camps have 20 sites each.

Princess Margaret Rose Caves Camping Ground
• 17 sites
(including 5 for caravans)
• 3 cabins
• Toilets
• Water available
• Fires in fireplaces only
(wood supplied)
• Permit required tel. 087 384 171

Pritchards Camping Ground
• 20 sites
(including 5 for caravans)
• Toilets
• Water available
• Fires in fireplaces only
• Permit required tel. 087 384 051

NATIONAL PARK & STATE PARK OFFICES

Angahook Lorne State Park
Lorne Work Centre
Tel. 052 891 732
Colac Regional Office
Tel. 052 335 533

Otway National Park
Apollo Bay Work Centre
Tel. 052 376 889
Lavers Hill Work Centre
Tel. 052 373 243
Colac Regional Office
Tel. 052 335 533

Carlisle State Park
Gellibrand Work Centre
Tel. 052 358 201
Colac Regional Office
Tel. 052 335 533

Melba Gully State Park
Lavers Hill Work Centre
Tel. 052 373 243
Colac Regional Office
Tel. 052 335 533

Port Campbell National Park
Port Campbell Work Centre
Tel. 055 986 382
Colac Regional Office
Tel. 052 335 533

Tower Hill State Game Reserve
Tower Hill Work Centre
Tel. 055 659 202
Warrnambool Office
Tel. 055 624 577
Portland Regional Office
Tel. 055 233 232

Mount Eccles National Park
Macarthur Work Centre
Tel. 055 761 014
Portland Regional Office
Tel. 055 233 232

Cape Nelson State Park
Portland Regional Office
Tel. 055 233 232

Mount Richmond National Park
Portland Regional Office
Tel. 055 233 232

Discovery Bay Coastal Park
Nelson Work Centre
Tel. 087 384 051
Portland Regional Office
Tel. 055 233 232

Lower Glenelg National Park
Nelson Work Centre
Tel. 087 384 051
Princess Margaret Rose Caves
Tel. 087 384 171
Portland Regional Office
Tel. 055 233 232

POLICE STATIONS

In the case of an emergency:
Tel. 000
It is a nation wide, toll free 24 hour service that can put you in touch with the police, fire brigade or ambulance. If for any reason a problem arises communicating in English, including emergencies, the Translating and Interpreting Service can help 24 hours a day:
Tel. 03 416 9999
Tel. 1800 112 477 (if outside Melbourne)

Geelong
Mercer Street
Tel. 052 253 100

Queenscliff
56 Gellibrand Street
Tel. 052 581 333

Ocean Grove
67 The Parade
Tel. 052 551 928

Barwon Heads
81 Hitchcock Avenue
Tel. 052 542 241

Torquay
18 Price Street
Tel. 052 612 006

Anglesea
Ocean Road
Tel. 052 631 377

Lorne
Charles Street
Tel. 052 891 510

Apollo Bay
31 Nelson Street
Tel. 052 376 750

Port Campbell
Lord Street
Tel. 055 986 310

Warrnambool
Gillies Street
Tel. 055 621 111

Port Fairy
Campbell Street
Tel. 055 681 007

Portland
Glenelg Street
Tel. 055 231 999

RACV – VEHICLE BREAKDOWN SERVICES

Geelong
Branch Office
23 Cavendish Street, Geelong
Tel. 052 214 122 (24 hours)

Queenscliff
Cliff Service Station
84 Hesse Street, Queenscliff
Tel. 052 581 841
Tel. 052 581 398 (after hours)

Ocean Grove
Ocean Grove Service Station
The Parade, Ocean Grove
Tel. 052 551 228
Tel. 052 551 050 (after hours)

Torquay
Surf Coast Auto
108 Geelong Road, Torquay
Tel. 052 612 002
Tel. 052 615 185 (after hours)

Anglesea
Anglesea Auto Service
87 Ocean Road, Anglesea
Tel. 052 631 302
Tel. 052 632 633 (after hours)

Lorne
Shell Surfside
70 Mountjoy Parade, Lorne
Tel. 052 892 593 (24 hours)

Apollo Bay
Apollo Bay Motors
Great Ocean Road, Apollo Bay
Tel. 052 376 720
Tel. 052 376 636 (after hours)

Port Campbell
Port Campbell Motors
Lord Street, Port Campbell
Tel. 055 986 351
Tel. 052 986 392 (after hours)

Warrnambool
Ed Ryan Auto Repairs
2 Walsh Road, Warrnambool
Tel. 055 622 112 (24 hours)

Port Fairy
Jago's Garage
21 Cox Street, Port Fairy
Tel. 055 682 700
Tel. 055 681 017 (after hours)

Portland
Les King Motors
135 Percy Street, Portland
Tel. 055 232 111 (24 hours)

Statewide emmergency
road service:
Tel. 131 111

RAILWAY & BUS SERVICES

West Coast Railway operate a regular daily train service between Melbourne and Warrnambool that stops at the following stations:

Melbourne ....Tel. 132 232
Geelong ....Tel. 052 266 500 (station 052 266 491)
Winchelsea ....Tel. 052 672 015
Birregurra..(only some trains stop)
Colac..Tel. 052 314 603
Camperdown ....Tel. 055 931 101
Terang..Tel. 055 921 989
Warrnambool...................................Tel. 055 614 277

A V-Line bus service operates along the Great Ocean Road between Geelong and Apollo Bay, departing from the Geelong railway station and linking with trains from Melbourne. There are 2 to 4 return trips daily, stopping at most towns. On Fridays (and Mondays during December and January) the morning bus continues through to Warrnambool. This bus connects with a morning train from Melbourne to Geelong and an evening train from Warrnambool to Melbourne creating a round trip that takes a full day. Enquiries Tel. 132 232

A regular bus service operates between Portland and Warrnambool.
Enquiries Tel. 132 232

Bellarine Transit operate bus services between Queenscliff and Torquay.
Enquiries Tel. 052 232 111

Further information and details on the above services can be obtained from the Public Transport Corporation. Enquiries Tel. 132 232.

SURF LIFE SAVING CLUBS

Point Lonsdale 052 581 257
Ocean Grove 052 551 382
Barwon Heads (13th Beach) 052 542 469
Breamlea 052 641 248
Torquay..052 612 335
Jan Juc 052 612 602
Anglesea 052 631 617
Fairhaven.......................................052 896 275
Lorne..052 891 724
Wye River.......................................052 890 297
Kennett River 052 890 277
Apollo Bay......................................052 376 765
Port Campbell................................055 986 275
Warrnambool 055 627 453
Port Fairy.......................................055 682 246
Portland & Cape Bridgewater 055 267 233

Locations and dates of SLSC carnivals can be obtained from the Surf Life Saving Association 03 534 8201

SURFING & CYCLING ASSOCIATIONS

Australian Surfriders
Association
Victorian Branch
Surf Coast Plaza, Torquay
Tel. 052 612 907
National Branch
Surf Coast Plaza, Torquay
Tel. 052 613 466

Cycling Organizations
Bicycle Victoria (touring events)
19 O'Connell Street,
North Melbourne
Tel. 03 328 3000
Victorian Cycling Federation
(racing events)
40 Errol Street, North Melbourne
Tel. 03 328 4391

TOURISM ASSOCIATIONS

Tourism Victoria
55 Swanston Street, Melbourne
Tel. 03 653 9777

Discovery Coast Tourism
Portland Tourist Information
Centre
Cliff Street, Portland
Tel. 055 232 671

Great Ocean Road Tourism
Authority (GORTA)
Great Ocean Road Tourist
Information Centre
55 Great Ocean Road,
Apollo Bay
Tel. 052 376 529

Shipwreck Coast Tourism
City of Warrnambool
Liebig Street, Warrnambool
Tel. 055 621 316

Geelong Otway Tourism
National Wool Centre
26 Moorabool Street, Geelong
Tel. 052 232 588

TOURIST INFORMATION CENTRES

Geelong & District
Geelong Otway Tourism
Information Centre
National Wool Centre
26 Moorabool Street, Geelong
Tel. 052 222 900

Bellarine Tourist Information
Centre
A Maze 'N' Things
Cnr Bellarine Highway &
Grubb Road, Wallington
Tel. 052 502 669

Queenscliff
Queenscliff Information Centre
Welcome Mart Coffee Shop
45 Hesse Street, Queenscliff
Tel. 052 583 403

Barwon Heads
Barwon Heads Tourist
Information Centre
Bodey's Real Estate
84 Hitchcock Avenue,
Barwon Heads
Tel. 052 543 100

Torquay
Torquay Information Centre
The Esplanade, Torquay
Tel. 052 614 606
Tel. 052 615 374

Anglesea
Anglesea Tourist Information
Centre
Caravan parked on riverbank

Lorne
Lorne Information Centre
William Street, Lorne
Tel. 052 892 709

Lorne Tourist Information
Centre
144 Mountjoy Parade, Lorne
Tel. 052 891 152

Apollo Bay
Great Ocean Road Tourist
Information Centre
55 Great Ocean Road,
Apollo Bay
Tel. 052 376 529

Port Campbell
Port Campbell National Park
Information Centre
Tregea Street,
Port Campbell
Tel. 055 986 382

Loch Ard Shipwreck Museum
& Coastal Information Centre
Lord Street, Port Campbell
Tel. 055 986 463

Warrnambool
Warrnambool Tourist
Information Centre
600 Raglan Parade,
Warrnambool
Tel. 055 647 837

Port Fairy
Port Fairy Tourist Information
Centre
Bank Street, Port Fairy
Tel. 055 682 682

Portland
Portland Tourist Information
Centre
Cliff Street, Portland
Tel. 055 232 671
Tel. 1800 035 567

Nelson
Nelson Information Centre &
National Parks Office
Forest Road, Nelson
Tel. 087 384 051

YACHT & BOAT CLUBS

Geelong
Royal Geelong Yacht Club
Eastern Beach, Geelong
Tel. 052 291 418

Queenscliff
Queenscliff-Lonsdale Yacht Club
Swan Bay, Queenscliff
Tel. 052 582 215

Barwon Heads
Barwon Heads Sailing
Association
Tel. 052 542 073

Torquay
Torquay Motor Yacht &
Angling Club
Fishermans Beach, Torquay
Tel. 052 612 636

Anglesea
Anglesea Motor Yacht Club
Point Roadknight, Anglesea
Tel. 052 632 824

Apollo Bay
Apollo Bay Sailing Club
Tel. 052 376 429

Port Campbell
Port Campbell Boating Club
Tel. 055 986 463 (bus. hours)

Warrnambool
Warrnambool Yacht Club
Tel. 055 628 233 (bus. hours)

Port Fairy
Port Fairy Yacht Club
Griffith Street, Port Fairy
Tel. 055 681 717

Portland
Portland Yacht Club
Lee Breakwater Road, Portland
Tel. 055 231 899

ACKNOWLEDGEMENTS

Tom Williams, Michael Sowry, Richard Cooke and Chris Bennett for their invaluable advice and assistance with all aspects of the production of this book.

Australian Surveying and Land Information Group (AUSLIG): for permission to use digital topographic data for the production of maps appearing on pages 6 & 7, 18 & 19, 30 & 31, 36 & 37 and 42 & 43, granted by the general manager of AUSLIG, Canberra, ACT. (These maps were produced by Mercadier, in Canberra, and the author)

Department of Conservation and Natural Resources: for permission to reproduce material from state and national park information sheets, and assistance provided by staff at park work-centres along the Great Ocean Road.

Tourist Information Centres: in particular those at Portland, Warrnambool, Port Fairy, Apollo Bay and Lorne for their help in verifying details.

Mitchell Library, State Library of New South Wales: for permission to reproduce the diary of Ernest Morrison's walk from Queenscliff to Adelaide. The original diary is held by the Mitchell Library.

Image Library, State Library of New South Wales: for permission to reproduce an etching of the Loch Ard wreck on pages 82 & 83.

Flagstaff Hill Maritime Museum: for providing the historical ship-wreck photo reproduced on pages 80 & 81.

Above: Angahook Lorne State Park
Right: Maits Rest

Bibliography:
Wrecks and Reputations
by Don Charlwood

Roads For The People –
A History of Victoria's Roads
by W. K. Anderson

Parks – Victoria's National
and State Parks
by Jane Calder